WATCHING BIRDS IN IRELAND

Guide to the best places to watch birds in Ireland

IRISH WILDBIRD CONSERVANCY

Clive Hutchinson

Published by
Country House

Country House is an imprint of
Amach Faoin Aer Teo.
2 Cambridge Villas
Rathmines
Dublin 6
Ireland

Maps based on the Ordnance Survey
and printed by permission of the
Director. Base maps copyright of the OS.

Text Editor: Siobhán Parkinson
Designer: Bill Murphy
Photographs: Richard T. Mills
Drawings: Killian Mullarney
Typeset by Printset & Design Limited,
Dublin
Printed in Ireland by
Criterion Press, Dublin

CONTENTS

WATCHING BIRDS IN IRELAND

There can be few hobbies which give so much pleasure for so little expense as birdwatching. The world of birds is fascinating and there is always something new happening to add to the excitement of this ever growing and popular pastime. One of the great advantages of watching birds is that it can be enjoyed in town or country, climbing mountains, wandering along the coast or just sitting by a window. Because of its geographical situation, Ireland has thousands of birds visiting its shores during spring and autumn. There are summer visitors from Africa, which come to nest here, and migrants from the far North, which spend the winter months with us. As a result there is no shortage of birds at any time of year.

Clive Hutchinson, one of our best known ornithologists, is the author of this excellent guide, which is ideal for the inexperienced person wanting to know how and where to go birdwatching. There is a wealth of information on what to look for during the different seasons, the best locations to visit and there is even a note on our climate. Also included is advice on choosing equipment such as suitable clothing, binoculars and reference books. For those who want to be more involved there are names of organisations to join and surveys in which members can take part.

I hope you all enjoy this wonderful hobby and I wish you many happy hours of birdwatching!

Éamon de Buitléar.

7

ACKNOWLEDGEMENTS

I am grateful to Hugh Brazier, Bobbie Reeners and Richard Nairn of the IWC for reading and improving the draft text and to members of the RSPB in Northern Ireland for advice on the Ulster section.

Thanks are also due to Richard Mills for a superb selection of photographs and Killian Mullarney for the drawings.

The Director of the Ordnance Survey of Ireland is gratefully acknowledged for permission to publish the maps.

Clive Hutchinson
May 1986

1 WHY WATCH BIRDS?

Excitement, curiosity, closeness to the wilderness are some of the reasons that people watch birds.

I spent a day some years ago on Dursey Island off the west coast of Cork with Dr Derek Scott, an English ornithologist, who had spent some days working on birds in Iran and was then living in nearby Castletownbere. Derek had spent many days in the previous autumn on Dursey and discovered that, although few migrants visited the island, those that did make it included a number of unusual species.

It was a warm, sunny day and we arrived at the rather battered-looking cable-car which crosses Dursey Sound just as the operator arrived. We stepped in and pulled the doors shut. There was a shudder and we lurched off across the dangerous sound. After reaching the island safely we set off on foot to travel the four miles or so to the southern tip of the island, where Derek had seen most of the interesting birds.

On the way we scanned the fields and looked into the few bushes that stand in sheltered spots but found no migrants. An islander stopped us on the road and asked if the birds were good: we discussed the weather and we wandered on. We passed the old school, a few houses and then the track twisted around the edge of a steep slope. When we came around the final bend we saw the Bull Rock and the Cow shimmering beyond the grassy tip of Dursey. A helicopter hovered over the lighthouse on the Bull and a small cloud of *gannets* flew to and fro. Other *seabirds* flew around the Cow. We crossed through the bracken and disturbed a tired *sedge warbler*, obviously a rather lost migrant, before descending to the grassy tip where *wheatears, meadow pipits* and *pied wagtails* ran hither and thither catching insects. We clambered across rocks to the tip of the island and watched the *seabirds* passing for a couple of hours. We ate our sandwiches and clambered back up the slope.

Despite our searches we found no more migrants here apart from a hummingbird hawk moth which buzzed past us heading foolishly for the sea. On the way back we found a *whitethroat*, a *garden warbler* and a *chiffchaff*, not much you might think for a day's birdwatching. But we had spent a day really alone in one of the most beautiful places in Ireland. We had watched some of the most truly wild birds, the *seabirds* which only come to land to nest, and we had lived in hope of finding an unusual bird. Even though the hope was not fulfilled we were well satisfied.

An interest in birds develops for all sorts of reasons, but for most of us it has its roots in a curiosity about the world we live in and the other creatures which inhabit it. There are only twenty-eight species of land mammal in Ireland and most of them are wary or difficult to see, but the most recent list of Irish birds incorporated 374 species. With luck and a lot of effort visiting a variety of habitats it is just possible to see a hundred species in a day and most birdwatchers will have seen about 160 species within a year and a half of taking up the activity.

Many of our birds are very beautiful — the *goldfinch, kingfisher* and *pintail* spring to mind. Others are drab and it is a challenge just to identify them — the shore *waders* and some of the *warblers* fall into this category. But all are different and the keen observer will notice how many of the characteristics of individual species are adaptations for feeding (such as the bill of the *shoveler* or the *curlew*) or camouflage (the plumage of the *snipe* or the *chiffchaff*) or some other aid to survival. Much of the fascination of birdwatching lies in the questions that it stimulates about birds' lives. Why do *tits* have such bright plumage? Why do some

Irish summer visitors migrate south to Africa via Italy, while others take a more direct route through Iberia across the Straits of Gibralter? Why are female *birds of prey* generally larger than males? Why do *Greenland white-fronted geese* raise so few young when compared with European *white-fronts?* Why? Why? Why? The questions are endless. As soon as one is answered another is raised.

The first requirement for a birdwatcher, even one who has a knowledge of birds' lives from books, is to be able to tell the birds apart. A good field-guide and binoculars are essential and a friend who knows birds well can be very useful. Unfortunately, many birdwatchers go little further than the identification stage. They tick off on their 'life list' the species they have seen and add up the tally. This activity frequently becomes competitive and 'twitchers' (as they are called from their habit of twitching all over as they wait for a rare bird to appear) think nothing of travelling hundreds of miles to see a new bird for their life list.

Rare birds are always exciting to see, but when rare bird hunting becomes an end in itself birdwatching enters a particularly barren cul-de-sac. Once they have seen a good sample of rare birds many birdwatchers who have gone the rarity chasing path burn out and lose their interest in birds completely.

Birdwatching can start at home in the garden with the identification of the common birds. Most people know *house sparrows*, *blue tits* and *song thrushes*, but surprisingly few know the *dunnock* which breeds in many gardens or the *redwing* which visits gardens in winter. Get to know these birds well and you will have a good grounding for getting to grips with the more difficult small birds of woodland and shoreline.

Curlew

This book will tell you where most rare birds are seen, but it is not aimed at the person who just wants to rush around the country seeing the unusual visitors. It is aimed primarily at the curious birdwatcher who wants to see a wide variety of species in as many parts of the country as possible. I will not tell you about the ecology of birds, though I will recommend some books for further study. Nor will I tell you what projects you can carry out, though again I will give you guidance on where to get further information. What this book will tell you is why Ireland is special for birds, what equipment you need, what organisations to join and where in Ireland you can best watch birds. I will not concentrate solely on the famous places where birdwatchers congregate in droves. Instead, I will try to pick out good places where interesting birds can be seen in every county in Ireland. At times you will feel these accounts of places where birds can be seen are unbalanced, that they emphasise some sites too heavily and that they ignore others, but remember that very little is known yet about the birds of much of the country, especially that part which is well away from the coast.

I have met many birdwatchers in Ireland. Among those I have seen in the field with binoculars are a former British ambassador (with Special Branch escort), a governor of the Bank of Ireland, a milk roundsman, a racehorse owner, a housewife or two and many students, schoolboys, farmers and office workers. There are even a few professional ornithologists employed by the Forest and Wildlife Service of the Department of Fisheries and Forestry, by An Foras Forbartha and by the Office of Public Works. The purpose of this book is to draw the reader out into the field to join this growing number of Irish birdwatchers.

Dipper

2 WHY IRELAND IS SPECIAL FOR BIRDS

The first thing you will notice if you buy one of the standard field-guides to the identification of birds in Britain and Europe is how few of the species occur in Ireland. We have only one breeding species of *heron*, only five breeding *birds of prey* and relatively few *warblers*. Even in autumn and winter we seem to get rather few species of birds. You could be forgiven for thinking that all birdwatchers should head for the Mediterranean or the Alps for exciting birds. Yet Ireland is extremely important for some birds and at times birds so rare occur here that people come from Britain and the continent to see them.

Breeding Birds

The following table compares the number of species breeding in Ireland with those breeding in Britain and shows that we have barely more than sixty per cent of the breeding species of Britain.

Because Ireland is smaller than Britain the climate varies less and the range of habitats is more limited. The location of the country, on the western fringe of the land mass of Europe and some distance from it, also reduces the diversity of breeding land birds. The scarcity of rich deciduous woodland means a scarcity of

	Irish	*British*
All breeding birds	136	208
Resident birds	107	157
Summer visitors	29	51

woodland birds as compared with the position in Wales, just across the Irish Sea, where *woodpeckers*, *tawny owls*, *nuthatches*, *pied flycatchers* and *redstarts* are all common.

The remoteness of Ireland from the mainland of Europe has had advantages, however, for certain breeding birds which have come under pressure on the continent and in Britain and have hung on here. *Choughs*, for example which have gone from England and have declined in much of Europe, remain common on the south, west and north-west coasts of Ireland where rough grazing of pasture continues. *Corncrakes,* which have been disappearing fast over much of their range, have one of their European strongholds in the west of Ireland. However, even here they are in decline and it is not at all sure that they will survive.

Wintering Wildfowl and Waders

In winter in Ireland, huge numbers of *ducks* and *wading birds*, and to a lesser extent *geese*, frequent our estuaries, lakes, marshes, floodlands and damp pasture. Consider just the number of *lapwings* you will see on a train or car journey across the midlands and then think of how many there must be all over Ireland. Look at any small lake or marsh and count the *ducks*, then think of how many more small lakes and marshes are scattered throughout the country with similar numbers of birds. The numbers of these birds are enormous and when extremely cold weather hits the continent they can increase dramatically. Attempts have been made to estimate the total numbers wintering in Ireland, but these estimates have been based on counts at the most important sites and probably understate the numbers scattered in smaller gatherings.

Ireland's location, mild climate and abundance of wetland habitat are the principal reasons for the country's importance for wintering *wildfowl* and *waders*. Because the country is on the western fringe of Europe we are especially important for wintering birds from the north-west, from Iceland, Greenland and arctic Canada. Some of the birds which breed in those areas, such as Canadian *brent geese, Greenland white-fronted geese* and Icelandic *whooper swans, golden plovers* and *black-tailed*

godwits, winter here in large numbers. Others, such as many *redshanks* and *dunlins*, move on to winter in England or farther south.

We also have a large wintering and passage population of birds which breed in Scandinavia, the northern part of the Soviet Union and, to a lesser extent, central Europe. These are *wildfowl* and *waders* which require ice-free wetlands and soft mud in which to probe. Many of the *waterfowl* — *snipe* and *teal* for example — have a preference for marshes and small lakes, which freeze over at higher air temperatures than larger lakes and esturaries. Each winter we have large numbers of birds originating from the north-east, and in exceptionally hard winters the numbers rise dramatically, as *ducks, swans* and *waders* flock across the Irish Sea to find a milder climate. These flocks fluctuate greatly, the birds moving off rapidly when the temperature rises again.

Ireland is a very special place for these birds, serving as a refuge in hard weather when they might otherwise die of starvation. For a few birds Ireland is important even in normal winters. For example, a large proportion of the world population of the *Greenland white-fronted goose* winters in Ireland. The importance of Ireland for these birds was recognised publicly twenty years ago when the World Wildlife Fund made money

available to enable the Irish Wildbird Conservancy to join with what is now the Department of Fisheries and Forestry to purchase part of the Wexford slobs as a reserve for the *geese*.

Breeding Seabirds

The fish resources of the Atlantic ocean are extremely rich and provide food for large numbers of *seabirds* to raise their young on the cliffs and islands around our coast. The availability of food would not be enough to attract the birds if there were not also suitable breeding sites, and these there are in abundance. The Saltee Islands in Wexford and the Blaskets in Kerry are the most famous. Other places like Rathlin Island, Lambay Island, the Bull Rock, the Skelligs, the Cliffs of Moher and Horn Head are also marvellous breeding *seabird* colonies, and all of them are dealt with later in this book. The Little Skellig, with perhaps 20,000 *gannets*, and the Blaskets, with tens of thousands of breeding *Manx shearwaters* and *storm petrels*, are exceptionally important internationally. There are few more exhilarating places than a cliff crowded with noisy *guillemots*, *razorbills* and *kittiwakes* and with *puffins* and *herring gulls* on the slopes above. The whole cliff is bustling with birds coming with food, feeding their young, avoiding predatory *gulls*, keeping guard, incubating eggs and generally carrying on all the active routine of birds which are intensely engaged in their breeding cycle.

Migrant Seabirds

Some birds do not stay long here, merely passing through in autumn or spring. Ireland is too far west to attract the great numbers of migrant land birds that occur on the east coast of England or on the continent. However, our *seabird* migrants attract birdwatchers from all over the world. Cape Clear Bird Observatory, off the west coast of Cork, is the most famous of the series of headlands and islands where it was discovered some twenty years ago that certain *seabirds* which normally feed well out of sight of land can in fact be seen from the shore in the right weather conditions. *Great shearwaters* which breed on Tristan da Cunha and carry out a huge migration around the north Atlantic can be seen every autumn off the south and west coast. *Sooty shearwaters* which breed on islands in the southern oceans and carry out a similar migration are often common off the coast. *Storm petrels* can be seen in huge numbers. Indeed almost any species of *seabird* can turn up.

There is something remarkably exciting about seawatching on a 'good' day in August or September. A 'good' day is normally one where the wind is force 5 or 6, the rain is pouring down and visibility is only a couple of miles. In

Gannet

these conditions parties of *shearwaters*, *kittiwakes*, *fulmars* and *auks* stream past on the south, west and north coasts and, to a lesser extent, on the east coast. In among these birds, every now and again, is something less usual: a *skua*, a *sooty* or *great shearwater*, a *phalarope* or perhaps a rare *gull* like a *Sabine's gull*. The very numbers of the birds illustrate the great richness and diversity of the oceans. The birdwatching can be extremely exciting as these birds can be very close indeed.

Other Migrants

Seabird migration is the most spectacular form of bird movement visible in Ireland. Migration of small birds is less remarkable. There are migrants of one type, however, which do attract birdwatchers in autumn from various parts of Europe and these are rare vagrants from North America which stray across the Atlantic in the autumn. This is the season when they are migrating in North America and they get blown across to Europe by westerly gales. The nearest landfall for many of them is, of course, Ireland. Most of these birds are the relatively long-winged *wading* birds which can be quite tricky to identify, but the most exciting are the small *warblers* which manage to make it across to Cape Clear or some other island or headland. They are easier to identify than the *waders* since they are usually brightly plumaged birds, but they are far rarer than the *waders*.

Location and Climate
So, as one would expect, our avifauna is largely determined by the geographical location of the country and by the climate. Our location at the western edge of Europe and surrounded on three sides by the rich seas of the Atlantic is responsible for our importance for wintering birds from the north-west, for our abundance of nesting and migrating *seabirds* and for the occurrence of strays from America. Our mild climate is one of the reasons that Ireland acts as a refuge for *wildfowl* and *waders* in cold winters, but the lack of variation in the climate — itself due to the location and size of the country — is a primary reason for the low numbers of breeding species.

Habitat
We can do nothing about the location and climate of our country but many of the habitats which birds use, especially those birds for which Ireland is special, are under threat. This book is not a treatise on conservation, but all birdwatchers should recognise that conservation of bird habitat is vitally important if we want to keep our diverse bird communities. Wetlands are being drained, bogs are being stripped, estuaries are being reclaimed, the seas are being polluted: all these things have an effect on the numbers and species of birds occurring in Ireland. We need to keep a watchful eye on future developments.

3 WHAT EQUIPMENT DO YOU NEED?

As with almost any other sport or outdoor activity, some specialised equipment is required to get the most satisfaction from birdwatching. Any birdwatcher you see will have two basic items with him or her — a notebook and binoculars — and one item — a text-book — at home or in the car. Some birdwatchers will also have a telescope and a camera but, unlike the first three, these are not essential.

Notebook

As soon as you become interested in birds you will find you need to take notes of what you see. At its simplest a well-kept notebook enables you to relive memorable days of the past. A quick glance through my own notebooks brings me back to a spring day when I was fortunate enough to join Oscar Merne of the Forest and Wildlife Service on an aerial census of birds along the River Shannon. I can still see the flash of brilliant blue as a *kingfisher* crossed the river below us and the flock of 16,000 *black-tailed godwits,* mostly in their bright rufous (red-brown) summer plumage, taking flight from the mud near Shannon Airport as the aircraft circled over them. We marvelled at the sight of so many birds gathered together before undertaking the long flight to Iceland to their breeding quarters.

A notebook does much more, however, than help you remember satisfying days in the field. It can be used for recording descriptions of unusual birds you see. If you cannot identify a bird make sure to record a detailed description of its shape, size, coloration and behaviour so that you can check its identity later. If you are carrying out a project, taking part in a survey (like the counts on the Shannon) or just out hoping to see something interesting, you will need a notebook to record your observations.

The sort of notebook you use does not matter greatly but it obviously must fit into your pocket. If you intend to transfer your records into a more permanent record book, then you hardly need a particularly sturdy notebook. I did this for years and have diary-type volumes covering observations for many years. However, I eventually tired of constantly transferring my notes, so I bought stouter notebooks and wrote my notes more legibly so that I could dispense with transcription. The exact form of record keeping you end up with is very much a personal thing: few birdwatchers use the same system. The main requirement is that you develop a system whereby you can rapidly retrieve any particular observations you are searching for.

Binoculars

Binoculars are your most important tool when watching birds. Take great care in selecting your pair; remember that the quality of the equipment may be critical in enabling you to identify a bird under difficult conditions.

The most critical things about binoculars are the magnification and the brightness of light transmission. Magnification is denoted by the first number in the description of the binoculars: 7 x 50 magnify seven times, 10 x 50 ten times. The second number refers to the object lens (the lens at the wider end of the binoculars): it gives the diameter of the object lens in millimetres. If you divide this number by the magnification you get a measure of light transmission and, for adequate brightness, this should not be less than 4. Thus 10 x 50 or 10 x 40 are acceptable, but 12 x 40 would give too dark an image.

Do not buy a pair of binoculars with a magnification less than 8x or greater than 10x. The lower magnifications are too weak for watching distant *ducks*, *waders* or *seabirds* and, despite what many books say, no advantage in woodland where

modern 8x and 10x optics can readily cope with the reduced light and closer ranges. Higher magnifications have the disadvantage that they are hard to hold steady and the more magnified image of the bird you are watching tends to shake in and out of the field of view.

The most common combinations and their advantages are the following:
8 x 30 – very light and used by many women
8 x 40 – usually heavier; better field of view
8 x 50 – heavy, but with very wide field of view
10 x 40 – generally light and compact
10 x 50 – heavy, but widely used by birdwatchers

Porro Prism and Roof Prism

Traditional binoculars are known as porro prism to distinguish them from a new design, roof prism, which has become very popular in recent years. The technical difference is in the location of the prisms in the instrument. The practical differences are more complex but I summarise them in the table. Preferences are really a matter of taste, but if you are on a tight budget you will probably get better value for money with a traditional pair than with cheap roof prisms.

Type	Disadvantages	Advantages
Porro prism	Heavy More three-dimensional image	Wider field of view
Roof prism	Flatter image Expensive Few external moving parts	Lightness Bright image

Manufacturer

If money is no object then buy the best, and the best, in the opinion of almost all birdwatchers I know, are *Carl Zeiss* (West Germany) and *Leitz.* Both now manufacture roof prism models only and their 10 x 40 binoculars are particularly magnificent pieces of equipment. They are extremely expensive but they will last a lifetime.

If you believe that you cannot afford to spend well over £500 or that you could spend the money more usefully, then consider the following suggestions:

Zeiss Jena (East Germany). Excellent optics and about quarter of the price of the West German version. The 8 x 30 model is relatively inexpensive and excellent value; the 10 x 50 model is perhaps the most popular among Irish birdwatchers. It is sturdy and bright, though rather heavy.

Japanese. If your budget is limited to the cheapest available binoculars don't despair. Most modern Japanese binoculars give very acceptable results, but be careful when selecting a pair and discard any with 'rainbows' around the image, loose moving parts or poor definition at edge of field of view.

Above all, resist a salesman's efforts to sell you what you don't want. Do not, for example, purchase too powerful a pair (you won't be able to hold them sufficiently steady once outside the shop) or a pair of zoom binoculars (they are neither as sharp nor as bright as fixed magnification glasses). Ideally, bring a knowledgeable birdwatcher with you.

Care of Binoculars

Binoculars must be treated carefully like any other optical equipment. Beware of the following hazards.

Knocks or falls. These can dent the casing and dislodge the prisms. The result can be double vision.

Scratches. These can permanently damage the lenses. Use a lens tissue to clean all the glass surfaces. Never use a handkerchief. The lens coating is very easily scratched.

Damp. Few binoculars really withstand heavy rain. Dark patches on the prisms or internal lenses effectively block out the image if the glasses are allowed to get damp. Keep them out of the rain so far as possible and, if they do get misted inside, let them dry out in a warm place. Do not fiddle with the prisms yourself as you may cause permanent damage.

If your binoculars are damaged, get them repaired professionally.

Telescopes

Most birdwatchers have no need for a telescope. However, if you spend a lot of time watching birds on estuaries or lakes you will find one invaluable for identifying the distant birds, or, if you are a counting enthusiast, they can enable you to count them accurately.

Despite the deeply felt love for the old family brass telescope still held by a dwindling few birdwatchers, there is really no question but that modern

telescopes are far brighter, sharper, lighter and easier to handle than the old brass models. Good telescopes are expensive, however, and I feel that money spent on a poor instrument is money wasted, as the owner will rapidly become dissatisfied with its performance.

At present there are several models which outperform the competition.

Optolyth 30 × 80. To my mind this is among the finest instruments available. The brightness and sharpness are superb, but the telescope does not have a zoom facility.

Kowa TSN range. These telescopes have a 77mm object lens so have superb clarity. They come with a variety of interchangeable lenses for different magnifications. Expensive, like the Optolyth, but superb quality.

Bausch & Lomb Discoverer 15-60 × 60. A very good zoom telescope, but less sharp and less bright than the two described above.

Kowa TS range. This range is approximately half the price of the TSN range and offers excellent value for money. Available with a range of fixed magnification lenses or a zoom. This is the most popular telescope among Irish birdwatchers.

There are several other good models available, but beware of inexpensive Japanese models with poor light transmission. And when you work out the cost, remember that these telescopes are useless without a good quality tripod.

Photography

An increasing number of birdwatchers are becoming interested in photographing birds. The Cork branch of the Irish Wildbird Conservancy (IWC) runs an annual photographic competition and the number of entries from all over the country increases each year. The standard too is improving, and the best bird photographers have their work reproduced in various journals in Britain as well as in Ireland. Our best known bird photographer is Richard Mills, a professional photographer with the *Cork Examiner*, whose photographs have won a number of prestigious awards.

Bird photographers nowadays depend almost exclusively on the single lens reflex 35mm camera and telephoto lens. Buy the best camera you can afford and seek advice from other photographers (not birdwatchers). You will need a long telephoto lens of 300mm or 400mm focal length. Even more than with the cameras, buy carefully, for the quality of your results will depend on the lens you use. Buy *Nikon, Canon, Olympus, Pentax*

or one of the other leading names. These are huge companies and they have a first-class reputation for quality products.

Some bird photographers use mirror lenses of 500mm focal length and upwards but these have the real disadvantage of a fixed and rather slow aperture. You might buy one in addition to a 300mm lens but not instead of it.

Even if you cannot afford a very long telephoto lens remember that some of the best wildlife photographs are taken with shorter focal length lenses. Heather Angel, whose work is widely published, has built a reputation on her photographs of birds and other wildlife in their environment. The subject is rarely overwhelming; instead, the bird or other animal is placed in its context. Such photographs are often more satisfying than a full-frame record picture of a bird.

In any event, you must get reasonably close to the birds. You can consider using a hide or stalking. A hide is easier and usually gets you closer to the birds, but stalking usually presents the bird photographer with an opportunity for more unusual action pictures. This is a matter of personal preference and most photographers use both techniques at different times.

If you are enthusiastic about bird photography you should read *The Focal Guide to Bird Photography* by Michael W. Richards (Focal Press). This gives a great deal of information on equipment and techniques and is based on the experiences of a former Royal Society for the Protection of Birds (RSPB) photographer who was also photographic consultant to *British Birds*.

Clothing

Birdwatchers wear all sorts of clothing, some sensible and practical, some very unwise. The principal requirement of footwear and clothing is that it should keep you warm and dry in all conditions. Wellington boots are essential for most of the year and thick socks should be worn with them. These can be uncomfortable if you are walking far, so you may prefer walking boots, but any *wildfowl* or *wader* watcher will find wellingtons essential.

Many birdwatchers wear denim jeans through the winter; but these are not warm and, when wet, can be extremely chilling. Thicker trousers are advisable. An anorak (over a heavy sweater in winter) is part of the uniform. Many birdwatchers wear ex-army jackets, but these are rarely very weatherproof. It is difficult to find an anorak which is both warm and waterproof and yet not prone to internal condensation. Among the best

compromises are the waxed cotton jackets worn by shooting and angling enthusiasts, but these are expensive. The very best, and also the most expensive, are jackets made of Goretex, a new material which keeps water out but allows the body to breathe through the fabric. I used to wear waterproof leggings but found that so much condensation clung to them that I was as wet as if I had not worn them; as a result I now wear a knee-length waxed jacket and wellington boots almost up to knee level. These keep me reasonably dry in the worst conditions.

Books

The first requirement for a birdwatcher starting off with an interest in birds is to be able to identify what he or she sees. To this end there are three excellent field-guides available. Look at each and decide what you require.

A Field Guide to the Birds of Britain and Europe, illustrated by Roger Tory Peterson and with text by Guy Mountfort and P.A.D. Hollom, is the oldest of the guides. First published by Collins in 1954, it taught me to identify most of the birds I saw as a teenager. The plates are generally excellent and the text is more detailed than in the other guides. In the latest edition all the plates are in colour.

The Country Life Guide to the Birds of Britain and Europe by B. Bruun, illustrated by Arthur Singer, was first published by Hamlyn in 1970 but was revised in 1986. This is an excellent and up-to-date book. Its main disadvantage is that the text is rather brief.

The Birds of Britain and Europe, North Africa and the Middle East by Richard Fitter and John Parslow, with illustrations by H. Heinzel, is very similar to Bruun's book with its illustrations facing the page, but it covers a rather wider area in Europe. This is a useful book if you intend to travel a lot, but the number of species covered can be confusing to a beginner. Published by Collins.

After buying a good identification guide you might consider a good book dealing with the distribution and nesting behaviour of birds as well as their field identification. The best one volume book available is still *The Popular Handbook of British Birds* by P.A.D. Hollom, first published by Witherby in 1958 and now in its fourth edition. I find this invaluable for checking points of detail about the nests, food or status of birds I have been watching.

Since you are birdwatching in Ireland you will need to know what birds to expect. You need to be knowledgeable enough to know, for example, that the all-black *crow* you might see on the Wicklow coast is almost certainly not a *chough*, since none has been recorded there for over a hundred years. There are five basic texts.

The Guide to the Birds of Ireland by Gordon D'Arcy (Irish Wildlife Publications) is a combination of field-guide and distribution guide. It contains colour illustrations of all the regularly occurring Irish species and maps of the breeding and winter distribution of many of them.

A List of the Birds of Ireland by Major R.F. Ruttledge was published by the Stationery Office for the National Museum in 1975 and contains a summary of the distribution of all species of birds known to have been recorded in Ireland up to the end of 1972. Although a little outdated, this should be on the bookshelf of every Irish birdwatcher.

Ireland's Birds by Major R.F. Ruttledge was published by Witherby in 1966 and is now out of print. It is, however, the most recently published book on the distribution of birds in Ireland and has substantially more material than the same author's museum list.

The Seabirds of Britain and Ireland by S. Cramp, W.R.P. Bourne and D. Saunders (Collins) is a readable account of the breeding *seabirds* of these islands based on a census of all the coastal breeding *seabirds* carried out in 1969 and 1970. The accuracy of the counts has been questioned, but there is no doubt that all or virtually all the major Irish *seabird* colonies were assessed. The book discusses breeding biology as well as distribution in these islands and includes some valuable maps of the main colonies.

Ireland's Wetlands and their Birds by myself, Clive Hutchinson, was published by the Irish Wildbird Conservancy in 1979. Obviously, I cannot write objectively about it, but I can say that it presents an assessment of the numbers of *wildfowl* and *waders* in Ireland and maps the main concentrations. Considerable detail is included on the best areas to see these birds and many people have bought the book purely as a guide to where to find large numbers of *wildfowl*.

If you want to expand your library you might buy books on bird biology, behaviour and migration. The Reader's Digest AA *Book of British Birds* published by Drive Publications contains excellent accounts of bird biology and behaviour. For an excellent and stimulating account of bird movements read Chris Mead's *Bird Migration* (Country Life 1983) and, for a good book on improving your garden for birds, buy *The Garden Bird Book* by David Glue (Macmillan 1982).

In addition to these general books you might read one or more of the books on individual species or groups of species which have been published. Three in the Collins New Naturalist Series are particularly good: *Finches* by Ian Newton, *British Birds of Prey* by Leslie Brown and *British Tits* by Christopher Perrins. Each is readable and gives a comprehensive and up-to-date account of the group it deals with. One English publisher, T. & A.D. Poyser, has specialised in books on birds and some are outstanding. Read *The Puffin* by M.P. Harris, *The Peregrine Falcon* by Derek Ratcliffe and *The Gannet* by Bryan Nelson.

Journals
To keep up to date with ornithological developments you should subscribe to at least one journal or magazine. They keep you informed about current developments and stimulate ideas.

Irish Birds is essential reading for any Irish ornithologist. Published by the IWC, it contains many contributions by amateur ornithologists. It includes the Irish Bird Report, which lists bird records of interest during the year, as well as papers and notes on all aspects of Irish birds. An annual publication, it is distributed by the Business Editor, Irish Wildbird Conservancy, Southview, Greystones, Co. Wicklow.

Whooper swans, Kilcolman Refuge

IWC News is a newsletter published quarterly by the IWC and issued free to its members. It includes a great deal of information about forthcoming meetings, conferences and other activities as well as commenting on matters of conservation and ornithological interest.

Local bird reports are produced for some counties and report on the birds seen in the area in a particular year. From time to time reports have appeared for Northern Ireland, the east coast counties of Louth, Meath, Dublin and Wicklow, for Wexford, Waterford and Cork. Support of these publications keeps you informed and also encourages the editors who face the difficult problem of selling sufficient copies to keep the reports financially viable. These reports are usually advertised in *IWC News* when published and brief reviews appear in *Irish Birds.*

British Birds is a monthly journal for birdwatchers published in Britain but covering Irish birds as well. Its editor is Tim Sharrock, an English ornithologist who was one of the founders of the bird observatory at Cape Clear Island. His continued interest in Irish birds is reflected in the amount of space given to observations in Ireland. Available by subscription only from British Birds Limited, Fountains, Park Lane, Blunham, Bedford MK44 3NJ, England.

There are a number of other periodicals and many of them are taken by Irish birdwatchers. Once you get interested in birds you will find your new friends more than willing to lend magazines and even books to those who share their enthusiasm.

4 WHAT TO DO

Birdwatchers tend to feel they should be doing something of conservation or ornithological value. A few treat watching birds as a competitive sport; these are the rarity hunters I mentioned earlier and they are a very small minority, at least in Ireland. There is nothing wrong, of course, in treating birdwatching as just another enjoyable pastime or sport but a lot of people, especially those who develop a deep interest, want to get more from it. This section is written for the really keen birdwatcher who wants to develop and broaden his or her interest or perhaps direct it into one of the specialised areas of ornithology where the amateur can still contribute much of scientific value.

Join an Organisation

The first thing to do if you are at all keen is to join an organisation. If you have read as far as this, then you must be interested, so write at once to the Irish Wildbird Conservancy, Southview, Church Road, Greystones, Co. Wicklow and ask for a membership form. The IWC is the only countrywide organisation catering for birdwatchers. Its very readable newsletter, *IWC News*, is described on p. 30. The IWC has sixteen branches, each with its own

chairperson and secretary, and there are several other groups which meet informally. There is almost certainly one in your vicinity and you will be given details when you join.

The branches hold meetings throughout the winter at which speakers talk about various aspects of ornithology or at which slides or films are shown. In my own branch we recently had a slide show on birds of Cork Harbour by Richard Mills, the well-known wildlife photographer, a lecture on a study of *mute swans* and a public film show. This is reasonably representative of the programme available at all branches. In addition, the branches organise outings to places of interest where beginners can see less usual birds and receive help in identification. Generally these are to local places but most branches organise at least one long-distance outing a year. Favourite venues are the Saltee Islands, Co. Wexford in spring and the Wexford Slobs in winter.

Membership of the IWC brings more than just the entitlement to receive newsletters or to attend lectures and outings. The real benefit is that it brings you into contact with those who share your interest. Within your own branch you will quickly make friends and find yourself on a 'grapevine' whereby news of interesting birds is passed rapidly from person to person by telephone. Perhaps what best illustrates the value of these contacts is the success of the conferences which are run jointly by the IWC and the Royal Society for the Protection of Birds (RSPB) in the Republic and Northern Ireland in alternate years. An interesting programme of lectures and films is always arranged but most people attend for the pleasure of meeting old friends and for conversation about birds late into the night.

So, for a variety of reasons, if you are a real enthusiast join the IWC. You will make friends, learn more and get an opportunity to watch birds in places you might not otherwise visit.

Chiffchaff

Co-operative Surveys
One of the advantages of being a member of an organisation is that it provides you with an opportunity to take part in surveys organised for amateur birdwatchers and frequently planned and run by amateurs. In the past fifteen years the IWC has organised several very successful surveys and these are continuing.

Bird Atlases
The Atlas of Wintering Birds in Britain and

Ireland by Peter Lack, due for publication in autumn 1986 (T. & A.D. Poyser), summarises the results of a survey of the distribution and relative abundance of all winter birds in these islands over the winters 1981/2 to 1983/4. The survey involved birdwatchers spending a minimum of six hours in each of the one thousand or so squares of the Irish National Grid, counting the birds they saw. It was a massive undertaking, but the results show clearly how important this country is in winter for many species which breed farther north or east. Many IWC members took part and broadened their knowledge of birds as a result.

The Atlas of Breeding Birds in Britain and Ireland by J.T.R. Sharrock was published after a similar survey of breeding birds over the five summers from 1968 to 1972. There are plans to repeat this survey in the three summers from 1988 to 1990 and, in the meantime, Ireland is taking part in a European Ornithological Atlas project which will lead in time to maps showing the distribution of each European breeding bird across its breeding range in Europe.

Seabird Censuses
Over the past fifty years several attempts have been made to census Irish *gannets* and *fulmars*. In 1969 and 1970 teams of birdwatchers tried something far more ambitious and visited virtually every mile of the Irish coastline and most offshore islands to count all the breeding *seabirds*. The results were published by Collins in *The Seabirds of Britain and Ireland* by S. Cramp, W.R.P. Bourne and D. Saunders (see also pp 27-8). The detailed figures indicate where the main breeding colonies were situated and provide counts of each species.

Since 1970 *seabird* experts have treated the counts of certain species, particularly *Manx shearwaters, storm petrels* and *auks,* with a more critical eye than was done at the time. These species are very difficult to census and trends in numbers at individual colonies cannot be seriously assessed without confidence in the methods used by the counters. In consequence, the emphasis is now placed on annual sample counts of several small colonies where five or six counts are made by the one observer each summer.

Unfortunately, few Irish ornithologists have carried out any sample census work and the counts carried out annually in the west of Ireland were made by staff members of the RSPB for many years. But there is plenty of scope for someone who wants to study a small *seabird* colony over a number of years.

Wildfowl and Wader Counts

Wildfowl and *wader* counts are carried out each winter by members of the IWC as part of a co-ordinated enquiry into the number and distribution of these birds wintering in the country. *Wildfowl* counts were first carried out on a systematic basis in the 1950s at a few important estuaries. In January 1966 an effort was made to count the *wildfowl* in all the most important areas and this was repeated in subsequent years. In 1971/2 a systematic series of monthly counts was instituted, covering both *wildfowl* and *waders* and including all major wetlands. Difficult areas to get at, like the Shannon river and estuary, were surveyed from an aircraft and other lakes and estuaries were counted by dedicated individuals who went out month after month for four years to census their local wetland. After 1974/5 the results were collated and written up in a book published in 1979 by the IWC, *Ireland's Wetlands and their Birds* (see also p. 28).

There was a period of respite from counting until 1984/5 when the IWC revived the programme. If you are interested in contributing to this survey of particularly vulnerable groups of birds please write to the IWC (address on p. 31) and ask for your letter to be forwarded to the organiser of the Wetlands Enquiry.

Register of Ornithological Sites

The IWC has collected a great deal of information on the sites of particular value for birds in each county. The files which have been put together have formed the basis for reports to local authorities on areas which are the subject of planning proposals and for submission to county councils on their draft development plans.

These files are constantly updated and information on newly discovered sites, especially in the midlands and west of the country, is requested by the IWC.

Single Species Surveys

In the past few years surveys of the breeding status of *mute swans, corncrakes, great crested grebes, choughs, peregrines* and *terns* have been organised by various bodies including the IWC. The organisers of such surveys are always glad to meet keen birdwatchers willing to help in survey work.

Bird Ringing

Bird ringing is a stimulating and exciting activity which combines the elements of sport and scientific study. The sport arises from the nature of the hunt which surrounds the effort to catch birds; the scientific study is at the heart of the activity which provides information of value to research, not just on bird movements but on life expectancy, causes of death and periods of principal mortality.

Bird ringing consists of placing a small metal ring with an address and distinctive number on the leg of a bird and releasing it. Any finder can then report the ring number to the ringer so it is possible to track the bird from place to place. For example, several *swallows* ringed in Ireland might be recovered in Spain in October and South Africa in January, indicating where the birds winter and pointing to the route they take in autumn. Alternatively, *ducks* ringed in the breeding season in northern Russia might be shot in Ireland in winter, indicating to Irish conservationists where some at least of our wintering *wildfowl* nest. The ringing of large numbers of birds in many countries over several decades helps us to build up a picture of the movements of those birds which breed in, winter in, or merely pass through Ireland.

At the beginning of organised ringing, the elucidation of the movements of migrants was seen as the main objective. Then it was realised that the recovery rate from large numbers of birds could be used to calculate the average life expectancy of birds and to find out how they die. Many ringers nowadays study single species, ringing individual birds, constantly retrapping them, measuring

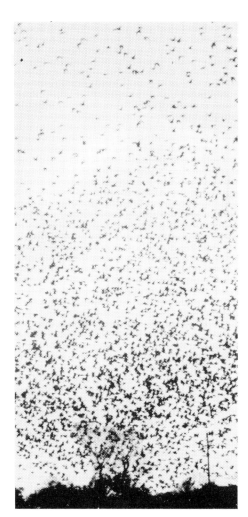

Starlings

and weighing them and recording their state of moult. In this way they can build up a life history of the species they are interested in.

Ringing is a difficult art to master, requiring considerable training. Under the Wildlife Act, 1976, a licence is required to catch and ring birds. The Department of Fisheries and Forestry, which administers the ringing system, requires to be satisfied that the applicant for a licence is properly trained. At present, in general terms, licences are granted to those who have satisfied the British Trust for Ornithology's regulations and ringed a very large number of birds under the supervision of a fully qualified ringer. Great care is taken to ensure that the welfare of the birds has priority over the enthusiasm of the ringers.

Catching birds can be a problem outside the breeding season. Fledgling birds are fairly easily caught in the nest and ringed, but adults have to be trapped. The most widely used method of catching is in 'mist-nets'. These are nets made of very fine nylon mesh which hangs loosely from tight strings stretched beween two poles. Birds are caught in pockets formed by the loose netting and get tangled in the mesh. Trainee ringers find these are not easy to extricate, but an experienced mist-netter can remove birds safely and amazingly quickly.

As well as mist-nets, ringers use various sorts of traps to catch birds. If you are interested in bird ringing you should get in touch with a fully trained ringer who is willing to train you. He will fill you in on the procedures you need to go through to qualify for a full licence. He will also tell you how much nets and rings cost and will give you the background information you need to decide whether you want to get actively involved. The most important things to bear in mind are that ringing is time-consuming and that most keen ringers find little time for general birdwatching.

Projects
Birds are very suitable subjects for certain kinds of intensive study to which an amateur can contribute and in so doing advance our knowledge of birds and open a new and absorbing creative life for himself or herself. Indeed, we in Ireland have particular reason to be proud of the amateur contribution to scientific ornithology. One of the great pioneers of ornithological reseach was J.P. Burkitt, the county surveyor for Fermanagh in the first forty years of this century. He placed different patterns of metal bands on the legs of the *robins* in his garden and so invented the technique of marking birds in such a way that individuals could be recognised. As a result he was able to discover new facts about territorial behaviour and song, to

observe threat display and to use ringing results to estimate average age. He had no formal ornithological training, but the work he did became world famous.

Few birdwatchers would expect to have such an impact on the scientific world but there are a number of areas where amateur birdwatchers can usefully carry out projects on birds in their spare time.

Breeding Bird Census

A census of the breeding birds in a limited area (town, large farm or small wood) can be extremely interesting, especially if the vegetation types are mapped as well. It can tell a great deal about the structure of the bird community, but the value of the project can be considerably increased if the census is repeated for several years. Then, changes can be noticed and the effect of changes in habitat on the population structure estimated.

Migration Studies

Study the movements of birds into or out of a restricted area throughout the year. Record the direction of movement and see if there is any correlation with temperature or wind direction.

Breeding Studies

Very few studies of breeding bird biology have been carried out in Ireland. Nobody really knows if Irish *coal tits* have similiar clutch size, breeding cycle and success rate to English *coal tits*. The birds look rather different and in Ireland the *coal tit* does not have to compete with the *marsh tit* or *willow tit*. One would expect some differences.

Scarce Breeding Birds

Some birds appear to be scarce breeders, but this may merely be due to their secretive or nocturnal behaviour. *Nightjars, barn owls, ring ouzels* and *blackcaps* are all probably less uncommon than people think. They tend to be inconspicuous, and so are probably under-recorded. A survey of these birds in a county or part of a county could provide much new information.

Roost Studies

The reasons that birds collect together in communal roosts at night are still not completely clear. It has been suggested that birds going to a roost can follow others back to successful feeding areas next morning. If this is so, a significant number of birds should leave in different directions from those in which they arrived. Counts of birds entering and leaving the roost from each direction would be of great value, especially if they could be related to the surrounding feeding areas.

These are only a few suggestions. For a good introduction to the topic and for further suggestions read Roger Goodwillie's *Projects on Birds* published by and available from the IWC.

Meadow pipit

5 WHERE TO GO   MUNSTER

Having developed an interest in birds you will want to see a reasonable number of species at an early stage. This entails visiting a number of different habitats, since different species occupy different niches. There is no point looking for *gannets* in an estuary or *wheatears* in an oakwood. But even when you identify the right kind of habitat you will still find some far richer than others. In this section I shall take you through the four provinces of Ireland, county by county, telling you where the best places are for watching birds.

Munster is probably the best province for seeing a large number of species, and contains the county with the longest list of birds, Cork. For ease of treatment I start with Waterford and work clockwise around the coast of Cork, Kerry, Clare and Limerick, and end in inland Tipperary. In general the coastal counties are much better known but do not despair if you live in Tipperary: there are lots of good bird places waiting to be found.

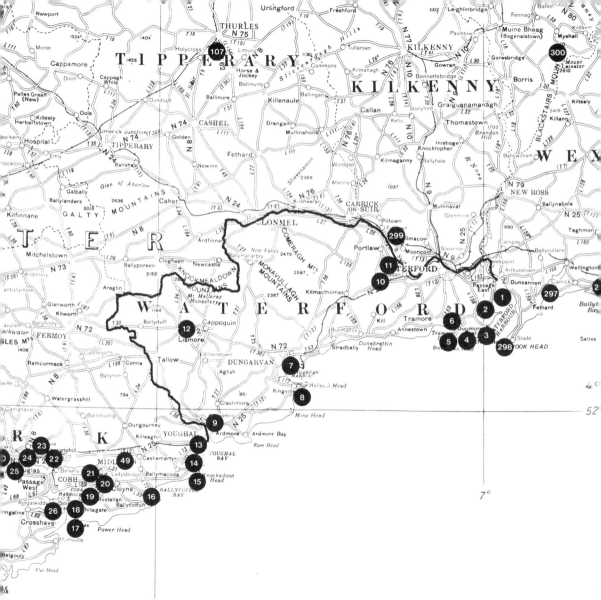

WATERFORD

Only in the past fifteen years has Waterford been reasonably well watched and the small nucleus of birdwatchers based in Waterford (where there is a branch of the IWC) and Dungarvan has discovered a number of good locations. As with all the coastal counties, the inland parts of the county are less known than the estuaries and cliffs, though the mountains are very interesting. For further reading try to locate a copy of one of the bird reports for the county produced in the early 1970s but now long out of print.

Waterford Harbour has a long stretch of coastline with several sandy beaches where *sanderling* are often found. Small numbers of other common *waders* occur along the shore. At Woodstown, north of Creadan Head, *glaucous gulls* should be looked out for.

Fornaght Bog, just north of Creadan Head, is a small coastal marsh with brackish pools and a good range of breeding birds, including *blackcap* and *grasshopper warbler*. In autumn it really comes into its own as a migrant feeding site and is well worth watching in the right conditions, following south-easterly winds. The bog is private property and should not be entered without asking permission of the owners who live nearby.

Dunmore East is a lovely fishing village with an extraordinary colony of over a thousand pairs of breeding *kittiwakes* on cliffs around the harbour. The birds nest in four groups, three of which are within the harbour itself. These birds are subject to a great deal of disturbance and are now very tame. Recently a pair built a nest on a lamp standard, but the surface was too smooth and the nest did not remain. *Kittiwakes* have attempted to nest on buildings and *herring gulls*, some of which nest on the cliffs among the *kittiwakes*, have successfully nested on buildings. *Glaucous gulls* visit Dunmore East regularly and *skuas* can often be

WATERFORD

1. Waterford Harbour
2. Fornaght Bog
3. Dunmore East
4. Ballymacaw Glen
5. Brownstown Head
6. Tramore Bay
7. Dungarvan Harbour
8. Helvick Head
   to Mine Head
9. Kinsalebeg
10. Ballyshunnock
    reservoir
11. River Suir at Coolfin
12. River Blackwater
    near Lismore

41

seen in autumn. A most unusual resident in the mid-1970s was an *Indian house crow* which had presumably been carried by boat. *Indian house crows* have a penchant for boat travel and are now well established in Egypt having reached there by boats from Aden and, ultimately, India.

Ballymacaw Glen, west of Dunmore East, has deep clefts with hazel and willow scrub which provide excellent cover for migrants. *Pied flycatchers, whinchats, ring ouzels* and other scarce migrants may be seen.

Brownstown Head, west of Ballymacaw, is another excellent migrant site in autumn and has the addded advantage of being a reasonably good seawatching site, though shielded a little by Hook Head to the east.

Tramore Bay is one of the outstanding birdwatching localities in County Waterford, having the largest *wildfowl* numbers in the county. A flock of 100 – 200 *brent geese* and 800 – 1500 *wigeon* are the main features. In 1978/9 a *black brant*, one of the Pacific race of the *brent goose*, was with the wintering flock. The mudflats also hold a large number of *waders*, the most interesting of which are over 200 *grey plover*. The bay is rather difficult to watch because of its great size. Approach from the town along the sand-dunes to get a look at the entire area. If the tide is high look through the *waders* roosting on the north side of the dunes, by the sea-wall. Watch for *short-eared owls* on the dunes. The richest part of the bay is at Lissalan on the north-east side, an area once reclaimed behind sea-walls but now flooded at high tide. The area is best approached from the road between Quillia and Cloghernagh.

Dungarven Harbour is another place for watching *wildfowl* and *waders*. Even bigger than Tramore Bay it has more birds and probably gives a better opportunity of seeing a rarity. The inner part of the bay is enclosed by a long, narrow sand spit called the Cunnigar. By far the best way of watching the area is to walk to the end of the Cunnigar as the tide floods in. *Waders* roost at various points on the Cunnigar and there is a richness in the variety of habitat which makes the area particularly worth working in autumn when American vagrants are likely. *Warblers* occur in the scrub along the Cunnigar at this time of year and parties of *finches* and *pipits* are on the ground. Outside the Cunnigar *brent geese* feed on the open beach from October on.

As well as the Cunnigar there are several other good places to watch from. Killongford bridge on the Cork side, about two kilometres south-west of the town, is worth looking over for *spotted redshanks* and the small pool on the left hand side of the same road just before the town holds a variety of *waders* in autumn. *Glaucous gulls* sometimes occur in the town. From Dungarvan follow the road out to the large factory at Ballinacourty Point. Look out for *grebes* and *divers*. Parties of *slavonian grebes* have been seen here.

Helvick Head to Mine Head is an attractive unspoiled section of cliff with breeding *razorbills, guillemots, black guillemots, kittiwakes, herring gulls* and *choughs*. Access is difficult and the birds are scattered along several miles of cliff.

Kinsalebeg is a small inlet on the Waterford side of the Blackwater mouth opposite the town of Youghal. At high tide it holds many of the birds which feed in Youghal Bay. A large flock of *wigeon* (up to 700) and good numbers of *waders* can be seen. Access is from the main Youghal–Waterford road or from the first right turn on the Waterford side of the harbour.

Ballyshunnock reservoir was formed in 1971 by the damming of the Dawn River to supply water to the town of Waterford. It is a good place to see *ducks* and *swans*, especially *whooper swans* which are quite rare anywhere else in the county. Several scarcer *wader* species have been found regularly, for example *green sandpipers* and *little stints*, and the

American *buff-breasted sandpiper* has been recorded.

The callows on the **River Suir at Coolfin** between Portlaw and Fiddown Bridge are the feeding ground for over a hundred *greylag geese* and smaller numbers of wild *swans*. The *geese* feed on two or three wet fields close to the river and are readily seen.

Somewhat similar callows on the **River Blackwater near Lismore** support large numbers of *Bewick's swans, wigeon* and *black-tailed godwits*. The best place is about four kilometres east of Ballyduff and the best time to visit the area is after winter rain when there is extreme flooding. The callows can be watched readily from the main road between Ballyduff and Lismore.

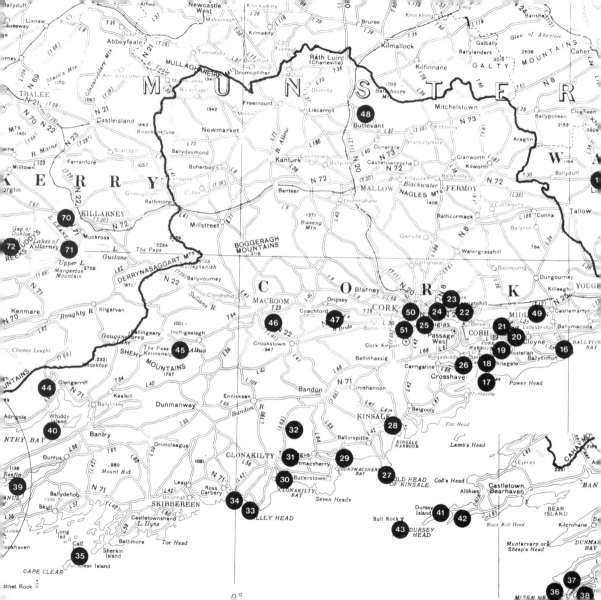

CORK

More is known of the birds of Cork than of any area in Ireland apart from the environs of Dublin and Belfast. The number of species recorded in the county is more than in any other Irish county and the local birdwatchers tend to be arrogant, because they believe they have the best birdwatching in the country. Because it is situated at the south-west corner of Ireland and because it has such a long coastline, Cork has a number of first rate ornithological sites. There is no book on the birds of Cork, though a *Cork Bird Report* has been published off and on since 1963 and Cape Clear Bird Observatory has produced a book on the natural history of the island. However, the local IWC branch is very strong and its members are knowledgeable about the birds of the county.

Youghal Bay, from Youghal Bridge south, holds some *ducks* and *waders* at low tide. These are the birds which roost at Kinsalebeg (see Waterford) at high tide. The place is worth spending time looking over for *gulls* and *terns*.

Ballymacoda Bay is a huge and rather lonely estuary a few miles west of Youghal. It is rather difficult to watch because of its size and is best approached from three angles. The first stopping place is Clonpriest Bridge where the road crosses the River Womanagh. Look at both sides of the bridge and consider walking downstream to see around the bend of the river. The move on to Clonpriest graveyard where you can gain easy access to the estuary proper. This is the best viewing place for the entire area. At low tide you can cross to the island in the centre but beware of the treacherous mud. Watch out for unusual birds: *spoonbills* have been seen here many times and several American *waders* have turned up. This is a good place for large flocks of *duck* and the flocks of *golden plovers* and *lapwing* can exceed 10,000 birds. Finally, having worked the main estuary, take the road over to Pillmore strand on the north side at the mouth of the estuary and look at the *waders* and *gulls* on the beach.

Knockadoon Head and Capel Island are only a couple of miles east of Ballymacoda village. There are breeding

seabirds and there is a chance of migrants.

Ballycotton, the small fishing village between Knockadoon Head and Cork Harbour, is the focal point for an area which many ornithologists consider the richest and most diverse in Ireland. No birdwatcher should visit Cork without taking in the place, and any day in autumn will see figures in anoraks with binoculars, stooping over flocks of *waders* on the beach or peering into gardens in the village. People come from Britain and the continent as well as from all parts of Ireland because there is always the chance of an unusual bird and there is the certainty of a wide diversity of species.

Start your visit to the area by driving down to Ballynamona strand and parking your car by the beach. Look at the small pool to your right and then walk along the beach to the two small marshes north of the car park. These two marshes have probably been visited by more American *waders* in the past ten years than anywhere else of comparable size in Europe. Just to indicate the extraordinary numbers which occur, consider that in one recent year two *dowitchers*, two *lesser golden plovers*, four *pectoral sandpipers* and a single *Wilson's phalarope*, a *stilt sandpiper*, a *buff-breasted sandpiper*, a *Baird's sandpiper* and a *killdeer* were seen at these pools. Rarities do not

just come from America. *Spoonbills, little egrets* and *avocets* turn up irregularly. Take your time over these pools. Do not tramp rapidly through them; sit and wait patiently as birds move in and out.

After working through the pools and surrounding marsh walk out onto the beach and search through the *gulls* and *waders*. *White-rumped sandpipers* more often occur on the beach than on the marshes. Rare *gulls* occur here, *glaucous* and *little gulls* being regular, and *Sabine's gull* has been seen. In summer and autumn there are usually parties of *terns* of all the common species. *Common terns* breed and *little terns* used to nest, but disturbance has driven them off. Walk towards the village along the beach until you reach the exit channel from Ballycotton Lake, then walk up to the causeway which cuts the lake off from the sea. The exit channel, which permits water to flow through the causeway to the sea, is often blocked by debris thrown up by south-easterly gales and the lake has deteriorated significantly as a bird habitat since the mid-1960s when there was an extensive muddy edge. The local authority concerned, Cork County Council, has been very slow to excavate the channel but the Forest and Wildlife Service, which established a no-shooting area here, has tried to reconcile the interests of birdwatchers and local landowners.

Despite the current high water level the lake is well worth examination as *ducks, swans, gulls* and *terns* use it extensively. In winter one can usually see *mallard, teal, gadwall, wigeon, shoveler, tufted duck, pochard, red-breasted merganser, shelduck, mute swan, whooper swan* and *Bewick's swan*. Normally there is a scarcer species present: *goldeneye, pintail, pink-footed goose* or whatever. You can see the eastern end of the lake well from the causeway, but to cover the western end you must return to your car and drive back to the main Shanagarry–Ballycotton road. Turn left for Ballycotton and then turn left again at the T-junction you reach after passing between two large reed-beds. About fifty metres from the T-junction you will see a grass verge beside a gateway which overlooks the lake. Stop here, rest your telescope on the gatepost and cover the upper part of Ballycotton Lake. Watch for *ducks* (*green-winged teal* has been seen from here) but also for *terns* and *birds of prey*. *Harriers*, when about, are best searched for from this vantage point.

Once you have covered the wetland areas you should check the pier for *gulls* or other *seabirds*. *Glaucous gulls* are almost always present in winter, *little gulls* and *black terns* in autumn. *Kittiwakes* are always present. The most exciting time is when large foreign trawlers come in at the weekend, gutting fish and drawing large flocks of *gulls* after them. In these conditions *Sabine's gulls* are seen every autumn. This is also a good vantage point for watching *skuas* and *divers*.

If you still have time to spare you should wander through the village keeping an eye out for migrants in the gardens. In spring and autumn quite a variety of *passerine* birds can be seen. *Pied flycatchers, whinchats, redstarts* and *black redstarts* are regular and rarer birds such as the *alpine swift, icterine warbler, barred warbler, yellow-browed warbler* and *firecrest* have been identified. The best conditions are after south-easterly winds, but hard work and patient watching are required for this form of birdwatching.

All in all, **Ballycotton** is a super place for watching birds. Unfortunately, relations between landowners around the lake and marsh and birdwatchers are not good because of differences of opinion about the proposed drainage of the lake. Please make sure, therefore, that you do not enter onto private property without permission from the owner and under no circumstances should you walk through fields of crops.

Roche's Point is west of Ballycotton at the mouth of Cork Harbour and well worth a visit to look for migrants. Being the south-eastern extremity of the harbour it forms a useful starting point for a tour of the area. There are mudflats at **Whitegate** with some *duck* and *waders*;

the shallow water off **Aghada** is the best place for *grebes* and diving *duck* (look out for *scaup* and *long-tailed duck*); at **Rostellan** the lake by the road has a variety of *duck* and small parties of wild *swans* in winter. Turn left at **Saleen** on the main Whitegate-Midleton road and drive around to East Ferry and Rathcoursey. Look out for *spotted redshanks* near Saleen and *duck* and *waders* at Rathcoursey. From Rathcoursey drive through Midleton and Carrightwohill, turning left at Cobh Cross towards Cobh. This brings you to **Slatty's Bridge** and Fota Island. Stop at Slatty's Bridge and have a look at the pool at the left hand side of the road. If the tide is in take the left turn on Fota Island and drive 200 metres up the road towards the large sand and gravel quarry. Scan the fields on the left hand side of the road: *black-tailed godwits* usually roost here at high tide. Having seen what is in the fields return to Fota and continue on to Belvelly Bridge. Turn left here and then take the next left turn again at the signpost for East Ferry. This road brings you along the edge of the 'North Channel'. *Avocets* wintered regularly in the 1950s and early 1960s. Where the water deepens look out for *grebes* and diving *duck*.

Once the road leaves the water turn around and return, driving back to Cobh Cross and turning left for Cork. Have a look at the muddy enclosed marsh at **Killacloyne**, just beyond the Elm Tree Garden Centre. Then continue on to the city. From the dual carriageway at Tivoli you will see some reclaimed land on your left where there are oil storage tanks and a ferry terminal. After passing the Silver Springs Hotel you cross over the railway line. Immediately after this bridge there is a left turn which brings you to the ferryport at **Tivoli**. Approach the terminal but turn left at the parking area and leave your car on the causeway. You can then walk across much of the reclaimed mudflats. Until recently there was a very large roost of *waders*. Nowadays numbers are much lower but you can see interesting birds. The scrubby vegetation also attracts a variety of species. In recent years *turtle doves*, *short-eared owls* and *black redstarts* have been seen.

The other good *wader* watching area of Cork city is the **Douglas estuary** on the southern side of the city. It was my own stamping ground years ago and that of many other Cork ornithologists. The estuary is readily accessible at various points. Its speciality is *green sandpipers* which frequent the drains on the edge of the fields surrounding the estuary.

The west side of the harbour holds fewer birds than the east but is well worth a visit. The best place is undoubtedly the lagoon at **Lough Beg** beside the large Penn Chemicals factory which has recently been established as an IWC reserve. The main interest is the high tide roost of *waders* and *shelducks*. Up to 400 *black-tailed godwits* can be seen in summer plumage in August. Access is along the causeway to the adjacent Penn Chemicals factory. The whole area can be surveyed from the causeway and a hide is planned.

The **Old Head of Kinsale** is probably the outstanding birdwatching location within 35 kilometres west of Cork city. Scenically very attractive with its steep cliffs and lighthouse, the Old Head projects farther into the Atlantic than any other headland between Hook Head in Wexford and Cape Clear in west Cork. As a result, it is a fine site for seawatching in spring and autumn and *great* and *sooty shearwaters, great, pomarine* and *arctic skuas* and *little gulls* are annually recorded. It is a better place for seeing large numbers of *arctic skuas* than Cape Clear. Indeed, I have been there when twenty *skuas* of all three species were in view simultaneously. The best conditions are strong south-westerly winds and mist. Rarities seen include two *black-browed albatrosses* (together!), *little shearwaters* and *Sabine's gulls*. In summer, when seabird passage is less varied, the large breeding colony of *kittiwakes, guillemots* and *razorbills* should be looked at. This lies to the west side of the head, just beyond the small carpark. *Ravens* and *choughs* also nest here.

The attractions of the Old Head are not limited to *seabirds*. In spring and autumn, when the winds are right, a good variety of scarcer migrants can be found. Search the bracken at the tip early in the autumn, then work back to the Speckled Door pub and west to Garretstown beach, looking at the hedges and gardens. But please do not walk on anyone's land without permission. I have seen *icterine warblers, reed warblers, yellow-browed warblers, redstarts, whinchats, pied flycatchers* and *red-breasted flycatchers* in this area. *Hoopoes, lesser whitethroat, tawny pipit, Richard's pipit* and *alpine swift* have also been recorded.

Kinsale Marsh, the small brackish pool on the Bandon road, about two kilometres west of the town, just beyond the Archdeacon Duggan bridge, should be searched at high tide for *waders*.

Courtmacsherry Bay lies west of the Old Head and is one of several similar west Cork estuaries. Work it from the road from Kilbrittain to Timoleague and out to Courtmacsherry town. One of the best places in Ireland to get really close views of *great northern divers* is from the town of Courtmacsherry itself. The estuary is fairly quiet.

Clonakilty Bay is the next estuary working west and it is generally considered the most productive of these inlets. An expedition here should include

49

Gullane's Lake, about three kilometres east of Clonakilty town, on the main Cork road, and **Bateman's Lake**, about a kilometre south-west of Ballinascarty. *Duck* certainly move between these lakes and the estuary depending on where disturbance is greatest, and *black-tailed godwits* sometimes move to the fields around Bateman's Lake as well. The lakes can be covered efficiently in a short time, but the estuary is vast and has two arms. As the road runs round most of it, access presents few problems. Look particularly at the pools behind the sea-walls which you will readily find when investigating the area. These have produced a number of rare *waders* in the past.

When finished in the estuary drive out to Dunmore and scan the open bay. *Surf scoters* have been found here in the past and *skuas* and *terns* should be regular.

Galley Head, west of Clonakilty Bay, and clearly signposted, is another spot worth investigating for *passerine* migrants. The list of species recorded is nearly as long as that for the Old Head of Kinsale.

Just below the head on the western side is a small lake named Kilkerran Lake which can be surprisingly interesting. At times it only holds a few *tufted duck* and *pochard*, but *black-necked grebe, smew, ring-necked duck, cattle egret* and *lesser yellowlegs* have all been recorded.

Rosscarbery is the last of the good *wader* estuaries west of Cork city and, for no obvious reason, has the least diversity. Nevertheless, it can be covered quite quickly and effectively from the road and is an essential stopping place for anyone travelling to west Cork.

Most birdwatchers have heard of **Cape Clear Island**, the island in Roaringwater Bay which has been the site of a famous bird observatory since 1959. The island itself is located about ten kilometres by ferry from Baltimore. It is quite large (eight kilometres long and up to one and a half kilometres broad) and has a population of about 150 people. The island is principally famous for the *seabird* movements which can be observed from the south-west facing headlands and for the rare *passerine* migrants which occur in spring and autumn. Almost any visit of a week's duration in August should produce *sooty, great* and *Balearic shearwaters, great* and *arctic skuas* and huge numbers of commoner *seabirds*. Although some *passerine* species have been recorded here and nowhere else in Ireland, the chances of a visitor seeing such extreme rarities are inevitably low. However, the island is an excellent place for a keen young birdwatcher to go to learn to identify scarcer migrants: *pied flycatchers, reed warblers, whinchats, redstarts, firecrests* and *turtle doves* are regular. Above all, the observatory is a place for a keen birdwatcher to meet more experienced ornithologists and to learn the arts of recording observations and careful field identification. Advance booking is essential. Write to the Booking Secretary, c/o Irish Wildbird Conservancy (see p.31) for details.

A glance at the map will show that **Mizen Head,** to the west of Cape Clear, juts out into the Atlantic in a similar fashion and should be an equally fine location for watching *seabirds*. In practice, it has proved as good as Cape Clear when comparative observations have been made, but it does have the disadvantage that watching must be carried out some 150 metres from the end of the head, because of the restrictions on access to the lighthouse compound at the tip. A visit to Mizen Head, however, can be combined with a search for *waders* at **Lisagriffin Lake** by Barleycove, where many American species have been seen, and for *passerines* at **Crookhaven** village where *red-breasted flycatchers, firecrest* and *lesser whitethroat* have been seen.

The two huge inlets of **Dunmanus Bay** and **Bantry Bay** have substantial winter populations of *divers*, mainly *great northern divers*, and Dunmanus Bay normally has a few *slavonian grebes*. The bays are very extensive but can be reasonably well watched from the road which runs around both. There are some

tern colonies in summer around Bantry Bay.

At the tip of the Beara peninsula, on the north-west side of Bantry Bay, lies **Dursey Island**, a remote place accessible by cable car, but which has proved to be a very useful seawatching site and, in autumn, an outstanding location for extremely rare vagrants. Shortly before the cable car for Dursey, turn left for **Firkeel** pier and walk across the field to your left to look at the overgrown valley beneath you. This is a wonderful place for migrants in autumn. To the west of Dursey are the **Bull and Cow Rocks**. The Bull has a breeding colony of *gannets*, numbering about 1500 pairs in 1970, and the Cow has nesting *guillemots, razorbills* and *puffins*, but both islands are difficult of access.

Returning to Cork city via an inland route, one can take in a number of interesting bird haunts. **Glengarriff Wood,** on the main Glengarriff-Killarney road, is a lovely oakwood where *jays* are numerous and *blackcaps* sing in summer. *Wood warblers* nested here in 1938 and the habitat is clearly ideal for them. The line of lakes along the River Lee valley is worth examination. In summer *great crested grebes* nest at **Lough Allua** and **The Gearagh**, the strange area of flooded forest about three kilometres west of Macroom on the Cork–Killarney road. The Gearagh is a fascinating place where

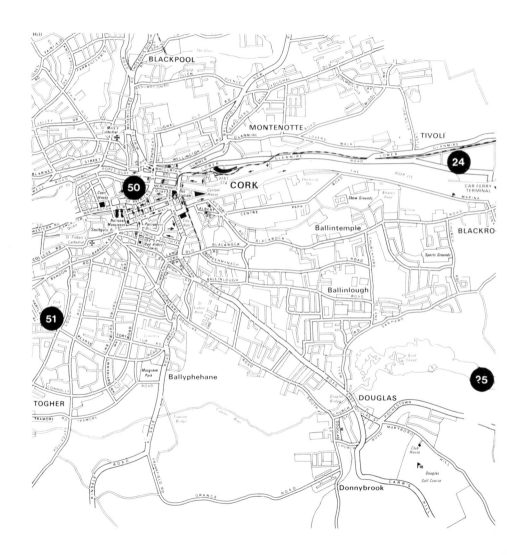

several thousand *duck* can be seen at times in winter among the partly submerged tree trunks. Before the ESB flooded it, this was a remarkable remnant of ungrazed cover typical of what could be found in much of Ireland before the land was cleared of trees. Nowadays, its water level fluctuates depending on the requirements for electricity generation and the area is quite heavily shot, but it is still a wonderful place for watching *wildfowl*. The stretch of reservoir between Macroom and Carrigadrohid can be as good, since birds fly between the two bodies of water when disturbed. Watch for *ring-necked ducks* from America here, as up to four have been seen together.

Between Ovens and Coachford on the same reservoir system, the small forest park at **Farran Wood** is well worth a visit to see an interesting collection of *ducks* and *geese*, mainly native species, in most attractive surroundings.

In north Cork, the most attractive place for watching birds is **Kilcolman Wildfowl Refuge** near Doneraile. This limestone marsh has one of the few bodies of open water in north Cork and attracts large numbers of *ducks*, mainly *mallard, teal, shoveler* and *wigeon*, and smaller numbers of *whooper swans*. The marsh has been substantially reinstated to its condition of the last century by Mrs Ridgway and her late husband,

Richard Ridgway. Mrs Ridgway lives by the refuge and should be contacted in advance by intending visitors (telephone: (022) 24200).

East of Cork city is a small lake on the side of the road between Midleton and Castlemartyr named **Loughaderry** which is always worth stopping beside for close views of *mallard, teal, shoveler, tufted duck* and *pochard*.

Finally, the birdwatcher visiting Cork should not neglect the city itself. The quays, especially **Lavitt's Quay,** should be walked to search for *glaucous* or *Iceland gulls*. Look on the river and on the chimneys and roofs of surrounding buildings. **The Lough** in the centre of the city has many introduced *wildfowl* but has attracted wild *black-throated diver* and *slavonian grebe* as well as *wigeon, shoveler,* and other common *duck* species.

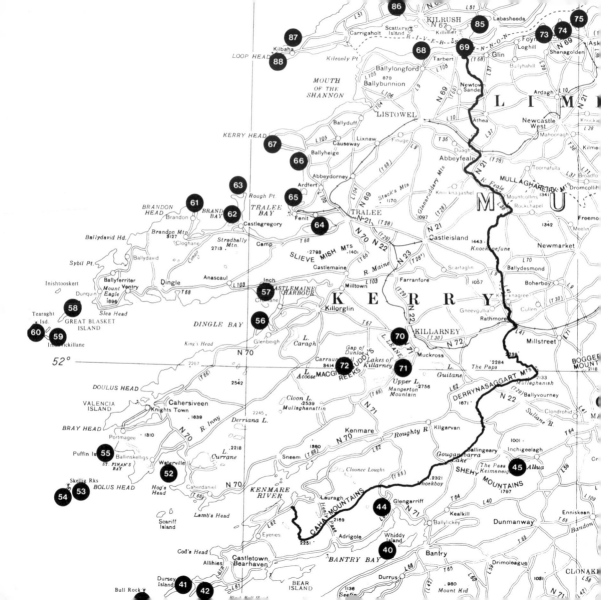

KERRY

Kerry is a large county with particularly well-known ornithological features: the huge *seabird* colonies on coastal islands and the regularity with which vagrant *ducks* and *waders* from America are seen. As well as these features, however, the county has very large numbers of wintering *ducks* and *brent geese*, and the bleak coastline and inland mountains harbour very large numbers of *choughs* and *ravens*, and a relatively strong population of *peregrines*. Birdwatchers are few but they know the county well. There is a branch of the IWC based in Tralee but as yet no booklet on the birds of the county has been published.

Ballinskelligs Bay, from Waterville round to Ballinskelligs, is an interesting bay for sea *ducks* and *divers*. *Common scoters* winter here and a careful search may disclose *velvet scoters*, or even a *surf scoter*.

The **Little Skellig** and **Great Skellig**, two rocks rising sheer from the Atlantic, are among the most important *seabird* colonies in western Europe. The Little Skellig has an enormous colony of some 20,000 pairs of breeding North Atlantic *gannets*, the third largest colony in the world. The island is an IWC reserve and landing is prohibited without a permit. However, excellent views of nesting *gannets* may be had from the boats which pass close to the island *en route* to the Great Skellig which has a landing place and a well-preserved monastic settlement at the top of an ancient flight of steps. The settlement was raided by the Vikings in the ninth century and was abandoned by the eleventh century. Nowadays, the walls of the stone huts provide nesting sites for *Manx shearwaters* and *storm petrels*, and the entire island is honeycombed with burrows used by the estimated 5000 pairs each of breeding *puffins* and *shearwaters*. A visit to the Skelligs should be mandatory for all who enjoy watching birds in awesome places. Access is best from Valentia where Des Lavelle, author of *Skellig, Island Outpost of Europe*, runs a boat charter service.

KERRY

55

Puffin Island, due south of Valentia, is also an IWC reserve but, unlike the Little Skellig, there is no restriction on day visitors. The island is a very important haunt of *puffins* and *Manx shearwaters*. There is no regular ferry but trips may be arranged with boatmen at Valentia or Portmagee. Landing is difficult except in calm weather and there are dangerous cliffs. Those intending to stay overnight on the island should contact the IWC for a permit. A leaflet on Puffin Island and Little Skellig is available from the IWC.

Travelling on the road from Caherciveen to Killorglin brings an observer along the south side of Castlemaine Harbour. From **Rossbehy Creek** at Glenbeigh on the south round to **Inch** on the northern side is an extensive area of some 10,000 hectares of mudflat and saltmarsh which supports up to 4000 *brent geese*, 6800 *wigeon* and smaller numbers of *mallard*, *teal*, *pintail* and *shoveler*. Large flocks of *waders* also occur and flocks of *common scoter* winter in the coastal waters outside the estuary. The area is vast and numbers of birds are difficult to assess, but the area behind the sand spit at Inch is worth concentrating on as this is where the *brent geese* tend to be seen.

Among the most famous bird haunts in the country are the Blasket Islands off the tip of the Dingle peninsula. This group of islands is famous in literature because of the books written by Maurice O'Sullivan, Tomas O'Crohan and Peig Sayers, three residents of the **Great Blasket**. This is the largest island and, although evacuated by humans in 1953, it has the least interesting bird fauna of the group. **Inishvickillane**, now well-known as the holiday home of Mr Charles Haughey, has an enormous colony of *storm petrels*; **Inishtearaght** has an even larger colony, estimated by one worker at around 25,000 pairs. Other islands have smaller colonies and between them the islands constitute the breeding location of a high proportion of the world population of this small *petrel*. *Puffins* nest in huge numbers on Inishtearaght and other *auk* species also nest in some numbers on all the islands. Anyone interested in joining a group should contact the IWC for details of any planned trip. Casual visits are inadvisable and access to the two most important sites, Inishvickillane and Inishtearaght, is restricted.

Brandon Point, on the western edge of Tralee Bay, is the place to visit if you are interested in *seabird* passage migration. Movement is at its best in strong north-westerly winds in autumn, ideally accompanied by mist. In these conditions *skuas*, *Sabine's gulls*, *great* and *sooty shearwaters* have all been seen on many occasions. But these conditions are uncommon and you should be prepared for quiet seawatching. The significance of the wind direction is that it pushes *seabirds* into Tralee Bay, which they leave to the west, passing out below Brandon Point.

Lough Gill is a small lake by Castlegregory strand which can easily be watched. Large numbers of *ducks* and *swans* occur in winter, and *barnacle geese* which winter on the **Maharee Islands** offshore sometimes graze around the lake. **Tralee Bay** and **Barrow Harbour** to the north constitute another large area of inter-tidal mudflat and some saltmarsh rather like Castemaine Harbour to the south. Several thousand *brent geese* winter here and large flocks of *duck* also occur. *Waders* are less numerous than at the larger Castlemaine Harbour. Both Barrow Harbour and Tralee Bay should be visited if all the *geese* are to be counted.

Akeragh Lough, a small brackish lagoon behind sand dunes a couple of kilometres south of Ballyheige, on the Tralee road, is internationally famous for the diversity of *wader* species recorded. The area is on private property but many of the wading birds feed on the beach offshore and can be watched there. Vagrants from North America occur so regularly as to be almost commonplace. *Pectoral sandpipers*, *dowitchers* and *white-rumped sandpipers* turn up almost every autumn and such extreme rarities as *stilt*, *solitary* and *western sandpiper* have been recorded. Scarcer European *waders* like *little stint* and *curlew sandpiper* occur here more regularly than at most other brackish lagoon sites in Ireland.

Kerry Head, north-west of Ballyheige, is another good spot for seawatching at the south-western tip of the Shannon estuary. Two bays on the Kerry side of the Shannon estuary are worth investigating. **Ballylongford Bay** and **Tarbert Bay** can both be watched well from the public road. As well as the expected *ducks* and *waders* on the mudflats, *grebes* and interesting *gulls* and *terns* should be looked for.

Lough Leane, the larger of the two Killarney lakes, has a moderately sized population of diving *ducks*, but the oakwoods at **Killarney National Park** are much the most interesting habitat. *Redstarts* and *wood warblers* have been heard singing in summer and probably breed thinly in the woods. Other woodland breeding species also occur in what are probably the loveliest woodlands in the country. Up on the **Macgillicuddy Reeks** which form an impressive backdrop to the town of Killarney, the hill walker will find surprisingly few birds. Breeding *golden plover* and *ring ouzel* have not been seen here for many decades. In winter *snow buntings* may be found high up. The only pure herd of Irish red deer may be seen on the mountains in the Killarney National Park.

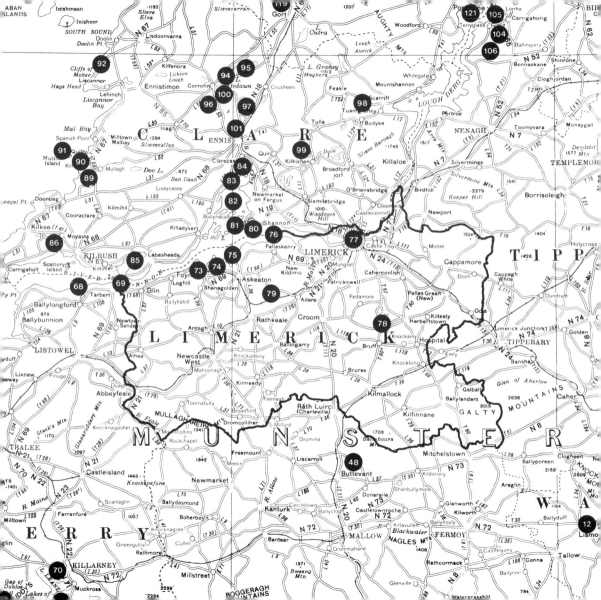

LIMERICK

Limerick's birdwatchers are fortunate in having the largest estuary in Ireland, the Shannon estuary, on their doorstep and their observations tend to be concentrated on the excellent spots for seeing *wildfowl* and *waders* there. An active group of local birdwatchers forms the North Munster branch of the IWC, drawing members from Clare and Tipperary as well as Limerick, but holding meetings mainly in Limerick. The branch has published two booklets on the area, *Birds of Clare and Limerick* by Larry Stapleton (1975), now out of print, and *Birds of North Munster* by Phil Brennan and Ewart Jones (1981), which may be obtained from the IWC.

Between Tarbert in County Kerry and **Foynes** the Shannon estuary has a very limited and rather rocky inter-tidal zone and few birds are recorded, but the numerous creeks and inlets around **Aughinish Island** and **Greenish Island** are the haunt of large numbers of *ducks* and *waders* in winter. Many of the creeks are difficult to approach and require considerably long walks on saltmarsh, but the whole stretch from Foynes to **Ringmoylan Quay** is a wonderful area of wild shoreline, only recently spoiled by the construction of a huge alumina extraction plant at Aughinish. The Shannon Wader Ringing Group has caught large numbers of *dunlin* and other *waders*. A small flock of *white-fronted geese* occasionally visits the area.

Limerick City can hold *glaucous* and *Iceland gulls*. Corbally in the city holds *whooper swans* in winter as do Longpavement Marshes.

Lough Gur, due south of Limerick, is the most interesting bird lake in the county and is an important historical site, particularly known for its well-researched crannog. The lake has a large *duck* population and is important for its numbers of *shoveler*.

Curragh Chase, about five kilometres south-east of Askeaton, is the best woodland in the county.

59

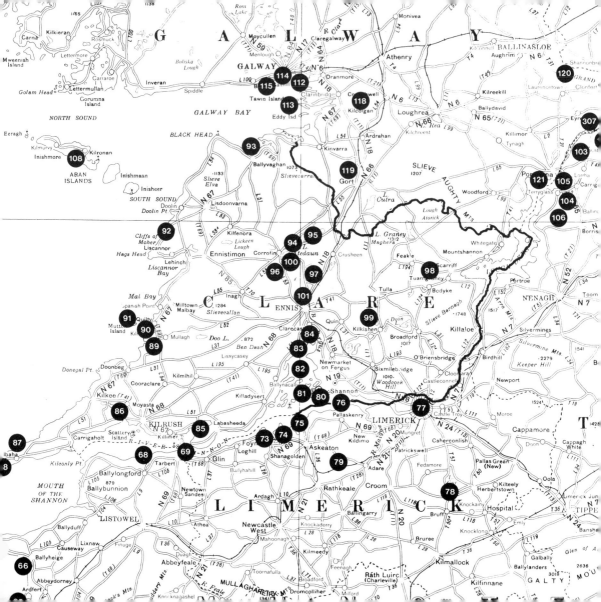

CLARE

Clare is a damp limestone county, best known among naturalists for the flora of the Burren. Although the Burren itself is not especially notable for birds many of the lakes on the fringe of the Burren and to the south hold wintering *ducks*. Years ago, *white-fronted geese* were common, but numbers are now much reduced. The north shore of the Shannon estuary and the coastal cliffs form the other major bird habitats. The North Munster branch of the IWC holds meetings occasionally in Ennis. The two booklets referred to in the account of Limerick bird sites (see p. 59) cover this country as well

The Shannon estuary is one of Ireland's most important bird haunts. Working west from Limerick city, the first section which can be easily approached is at **Shannon Airport**. The mudflats at Shannon, Rineanna and Deenish Island hold large numbers of *wigeon* and *teal* and lesser numbers of *mallard*, *shoveler*, *shelduck* and *scaup*. Up to 5000 *black-tailed godwits*, 15,000 *dunlin* and 5000 *knot* have been counted here on many occasions. The shoreline can be approached at a number of points from Shannon town. **Shannon Airport lagoon**, a small enclosed lagoon at the airport, is on private property and access is prohibited without special permission for security reasons. The lagoon has a small *wildfowl* population in winter, often including some wild *swans*, and can attract scarce passing *waders* in autumn. American species such as *pectoral* and *white-rumped sandpipers* have been recorded. A substantial number of birds have been caught in the reed-beds here and ringed, mostly as part of a long-term study of *sedge warblers*. *Grasshopper warblers* also occur here and Ireland's first recorded *Savi's warbler* was trapped at the lagoon. Please do not visit the area, however, without permission from Aer Rianta, the airport authority.

The **Fergus estuary** is the broad arm of the Shannon estuary north of a line from Shannon across to Killadysert. The whole area of mudflat is enormous and

CLARE

very difficult to watch, but the spectacle of tens of thousands of *waders* following the ebbing tide over 20 square kilometres of mudflat is unparalleled in the country. A number of small roads lead down to the estuary, one of the best being the laneway to Ing and the small hillock there which forms an ideal vantage point for watching birds moving out with the tide. The west side of the estuary can be approached at **Islandavanna** and **Islandmagrath**: be prepared for a substantial walk.

This estuary is so large that it is difficult to understand how monthly counts of the *wildfowl* and *waders* of the entire Shannon estuary were carried out in January 1973 and during the winters from 1973/4 to 1976/7. In fact, only the January 1973 census was carried out by birdwatchers on the ground: the other counts were carried out from a light aircraft flying at low altitude. The aerial counts ceased after an Irish Air Corps aircraft accidentally hit the water south of the Fergus estuary and sank; luckily, Oscar Merne, the observer, and the pilot were able to swim to safety. By then the counts had achieved their main objective of providing seasonal totals for all the *wildfowl* and *waders* in the estuary and establishing the internationally important status of the area. A repeat ground count would be a useful exercise after so many years without counts, but the difficulty of covering both sides of an 80 kilometre

long estuary is enormous. The 1973 count involved teams of four counters on each side of the estuary and took two full days of hard work. Nevertheless, the effort all seemed worthwhile when we sat down in the evening to total up the figures.

Clonderalaw Bay between Labasheeda and Killadysert on the Shannon estuary has a shoreline with some *ducks* and *waders*, but is not so good as **Poulnasherry Bay**, farther west, where a flock of several hundred *brent geese* winters. Other *wildfowl* species, including *scaup*, also occur. Both bays can be approached at a number of points.

Bridges of Ross, almost at Loop Head, has proved to be a superb seawatching site in recent years with large movements of most *seabirds*. It is one of the best places to see *Leach's petrels* and, of course, *storm petrels* can also be seen in autumn. Beware, however, if you have not tried seawatching before, as it can be extremely difficult to see some of these birds before getting your eye in with practice. **Loop Head** has a large colony of nesting seabirds with 3000–5000 *guillemots* and a handful of *puffins*.

Several places on the west coast of Clare are worth a visit if you are in the area. **Lough Donnell**, south of Mullagh, is an attractive small lagoon which looks as though it should hold rare *waders* but has actually produced remarkably little. **Lurga Point** opposite **Mutton Island** has a winter population of *purple sandpipers* and provides opportunities for looking across at the *barnacle geese* on Mutton Island. The **Cliffs of Moher**, west of Ennistimon, are among the most magnificent cliffs in the country and provide a wonderful setting for watching *guillemots, razorbills* and *puffins*. It is one of the most readily accessible places in the country where *puffins* can be seen well. *Choughs* and *ravens* also breed. The visitor centre in the carpark near the cliffs has a display of mounted *seabirds*. The manager is knowledgeable about birds and will give local directions.

Ballyvaughan Bay, north of the Burren, on the south side of Galway Bay, is technically in County Clare, but is really an extension of Galway Bay and many of the birds which occur there, such as *brent geese*, can be seen in larger numbers on the Galway side of the county boundary. Do not travel from the Cliffs of Moher to Ballyvaughan with blinkered eyes. If birds are few, the flowers and archaeological remains are spectacular.

Many of the Clare lakes hold *wigeon, teal, mallard* and other *duck*. **Ballyeighter Loughs, Lough Cullaun, Ballycullinan Lough, Dromore Lough, Lough O'Grady** and **Lough Cullaunyheeda** are all of interest, but two lakes stand out. **Lough**

Atedaun, a kilometre east of Corrofin, is a lovely wild shallow lake where flocks of *whooper* and *Bewick's swans* occur and quite large numbers of *wigeon* can be seen. **Ballyallia Lake** near Ennis is one of my favourite *wildfowl* lakes in the country. Quite a small lake, it has an attractive wood on one side and a popular carpark on another and is frequented by Ennis peope as a local amenity. The lake provides ready viewing of all the common species of dabbling *duck* and several species of diving *duck*. The largest flock of *gadwall* in Ireland winters here. Both *whooper* and *Bewick's swans* occur in small numbers in winter and *great crested grebes* can be seen in summer. The lake can be easily watched from the carpark and from the narrow road on the south side of the lake which leads to a small round tower. Travel the full length of this road to see the farthest western arm of the lake.

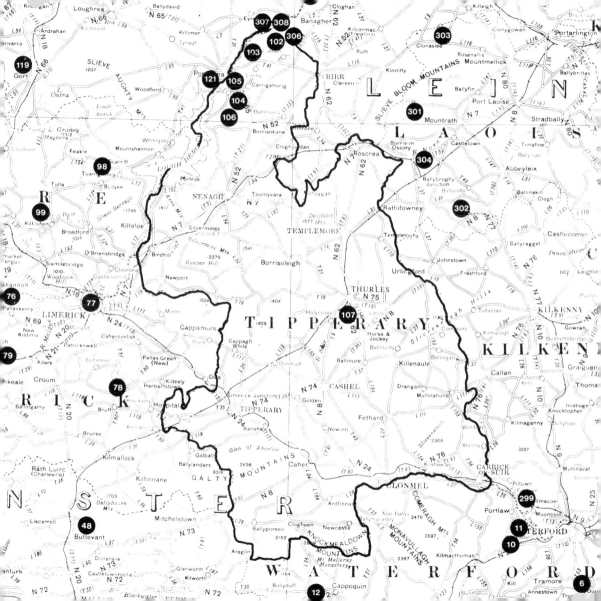

TIPPERARY

Although one of the largest Irish counties, Tipperary is relatively unknown for its birds. The west shore of Lough Derg and the south shore of the Little Brosna are probably the best-known bird haunts. There are others, however, and they need to be worked seriously.

The **Little Brosna** and the **River Shannon** mark the north-west boundary of the county and are wonderful *wildfowl* haunts, but the Little Brosna is much more easily approached from the Offaly side and the Shannon from the Galway side. See the accounts of the birdwatching sites in these counties for more details.

Redfern Lough on the left hand side of the road from Borrisokane to Terryglass is a turlough surrounded by meadows which are prone to flood and attract *wildfowl*, including small numbers of *whooper* and *Bewick's swans* and, at times, *white-fronted geese.*

Slevoir Bay in the north-eastern corner of Lough Derg is probably the most interesting portion of the lough in County Tipperary. Good numbers of diving *duck* occur and *white-fronted geese* also frequent this area. There is some deciduous woodland on the southern shore which would repay visiting.

Lough Avan, some six kilometres west of Borrisokane, is another small lake where *white-fronted geese* sometimes occur.

Thurles sugar factory lagoon is a marvellous place, totally surprising when one comes suddenly on it near the sugar factory at Thurles about four kilometres south-south-west of the town. Thousands of *duck* winter here and in autumn passage *waders* and even *black terns* have been seen. The whole area is quite remarkably rich at all seasons. *Green sandpipers* appear to be present almost permanently.

TIPPERARY

102. Little Brosna
103. River Shannon
104. Redfern Lough
105. Slevoir Bay
106. Lough Avan
107. Thurles
     sugar factory
     lagoon

CONNACHT

Connacht has a long and rugged
coastline with deep bays, a number of
islands and few estuaries. Inland it is
dominated by the large Lough Conn,
Lough Mask and Lough Corrib, in the
north-west by the extent of blanket bog
and in the east by the vast areas of
floodland which provide security for
ducks and certain *waders*. The best bird
areas were identified years ago by two
great Irish ornithologists who made this
province their home. Robert Warren,
who lived in Sligo on the shore of Killala
Bay, learned much of the birds of north
Connacht in the second half of the
nineteenth century and, in the present
century, Major R.F. Ruttledge while
living on the shore of Lough Carra
explored all the islands off the coast and
the turloughs and lakes inland.

There are fewer very important bird sites
in Connacht than in the other provinces
so this section will be quite short. The
coastal counties are dealt with first and
then the inland ones: Galway, Mayo,
Sligo, Leitrim and Roscommon.

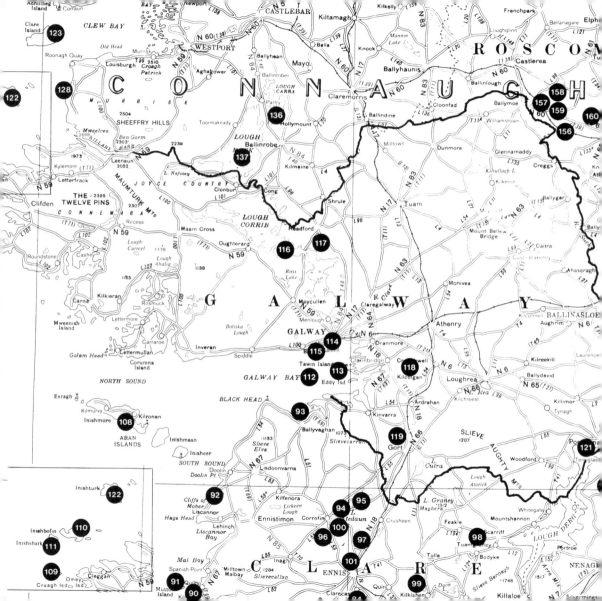

GALWAY

There is a strong branch of the Irish Wildbird Conservancy centred on Galway and its members have kept our knowledge of the birds up to date by surveying the lakes and much of the coastline. *The Birds of Galway and Mayo* by Tony Whilde, first published in 1977 by the IWC and since reprinted, is essential for the visitor. As well as a systematic list of birds recorded it includes an invaluable list of the bird habitats, much more than I have room for, but on which I have drawn for this account. Tony Whilde is a professional ecologist who runs the Corrib Conservation Centre at Rosscahill and has published extensively on the birds of Galway and Mayo.

The **Aran Islands** in Galway Bay are the only islands served by CIE, but the numbers and diversity of birds are lower than at other Galway islands. *Kittiwakes* nest in some numbers, but an interest in birds would not be my principal reason for visiting the islands. Farther north, **High Island,** uninhabited and owned by the poet, Richard Murphy, holds breeding *storm petrels* and *Manx shearwaters* but access is difficult. Off Cleggan, beyond Clifden, lie **Inishbofin** and **Inishshark,** two islands which have been quite well studied over the past fifty years. Inishshark is now uninhabited and has spectacular cliffs with small numbers of cliff-breeding *seabirds*. Inishbofin, a lovely island with a resilient human population, still has nesting *corncrakes* and *corn buntings* in the small fields. Numbers of *corncrakes* have fallen, though, since the years when one observer described them as uncountable at night with craking on all sides. Even in recent years I have heard six craking from a bedroom window on the island. In the late 1950s a couple of birdwatchers spent the late autumn on Inishbofin watching migrants and found that the island attracted a variety of species but in small numbers.

The coastline of Galway, though lengthy, does not have many cliffs for breeding *seabirds* or muddy estuaries for *wildfowl*. **Galway Bay** itself has much the largest area of feeding for *ducks* and *waders*.

GALWAY

Follow the road out to **Tawin Island** for the best vantage point. In winter *brent geese* can be seen, together with *wigeon, oystercatchers, grey plovers, redshanks* and other *waders*. The seals are also well worth watching here. Work back from Tawin to Galway city and drive down to **Nimmo's Pier** at the Claddagh. This unprepossessing site is an excellent place for watching *waders* and the *gulls* and *divers* which drift in and out of the bay. There are almost always *glaucous gulls* here and, frequently, *little gulls*. After strong winds this could attract storm-blown *seabirds* from anywhere in the north-west North Atlantic. West of Galway Bay is **Rusheen Bay** near Barna, for many years a bird sanctuary and in summer a fine place for watching *terns*. *Waders* can also be watched here, often at quite close range.

The road west from Galway city is frequently considered to be very poor for birds. Appearances can belie the truth, however. I recall a contest between two groups of birdwatchers one November following a conference on birds in Galway. The object was to see which group could find the largest number of species in a ten kilometre square of the National Grid west of Barna. Some sceptics considered it would be impossible to find twenty-five species. In fact, a total of over fifty species was found by the two groups, including such unusual birds as *hen harrier* and *chiffchaff*.

Perhaps such a story could be told about other parts of Ireland, but clearly the Galway coast should be looked at closely by the birdwatcher.

Inland, the main attraction in Galway is its wetlands. **Lough Corrib** is the second largest lake in the country and, because of its size, is difficult to watch. In summer, the islands have large colonies of nesting *common, black-headed, herring* and *lesser black-backed gulls* as well as breeding *terns, great crested grebes, tufted ducks* and *red-breasted mergansers*. In late autumn enormous numbers of *pochard* and *coots* visit the lower lake. From Angliham marble quarries the flock appears like a huge raft, but to assess the numbers overflying by aircraft is essential. Estimates of up to 21,000 *pochard*, 5000 *tufted ducks* and 11,000 *coots* have been made. At the Mount Ross inlet *gadwall* can be seen in winter.

Rostaff Lake near Headford has a hide, run by the IWC Galway branch, where *white-fronted geese* and *ducks* may be seen in winter.

Rahasane turlough near Craughwell, just east of the Limerick-Galway road, is the other internationally important wetland in Galway. The Dunkellin river floods in autumn and forms a broad, shallow lake at Rahasane providing a secure food resource for 6000 *ducks* and wild *swans*. Whether the lake is a true turlough is a matter of some dispute; however, the vegetation is typical of turlough vegetation in the west of Ireland. The lake is best watched from the road running parallel to the Dunkellin river. Large numbers of *wigeon* and *teal* and smaller numbers of *mallard, shoveler* and *pintail* are usually present, together with small parties of *Bewick's, whooper* and *mute swans*. At times, perhaps because of heavy shooting or because the water level is too high, the lake can have only a handful of birds. This was formerly a place where *white-fronted geese* could always be found in winter. Nowadays they are far less regular.

Farther south, the woods and lake at **Coole** are now a State nature reserve and can be visited at any season with profit. In winter, there are wild *swans* to be seen and in summer the woodland is rich with breeding birds.

The eastern side of the county is bounded by the **River Suck,** the River Shannon and part of Lough Derg. The Suck floods, though not so extensively as the Little Brosna in Offaly, and the callows hold flocks of *wigeon, teal,* wild *swans* and *golden plovers*. The Shannon has similar flocks. At **Portumna,** the Forest and Wildlife Service has created a most successful sanctuary where flocks of *mallard* congregate to moult. In summer there are good views of the nesting *cormorants*.

Flock of waders in flight

71

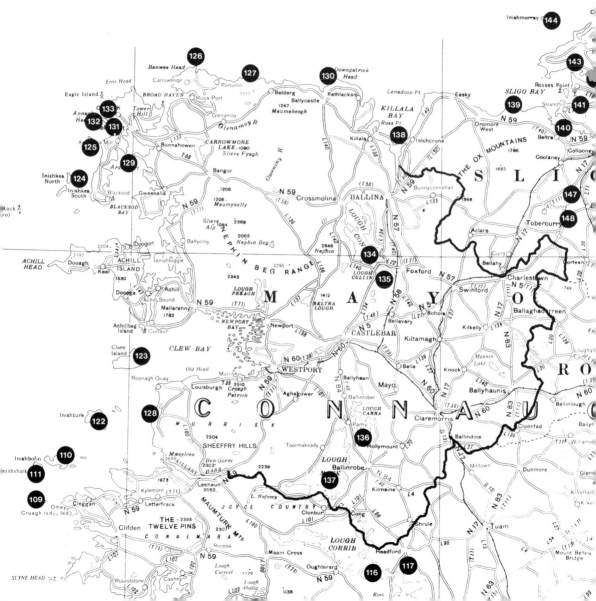

MAYO

Mayo has even fewer birdwatchers than Galway to cover a huge county, but there is now a Mayo branch of the IWC and *The Birds of Galway and Mayo* by Tony Whilde provides a remarkably thorough account of the birds and includes summaries of the principal habitats.

Inishturk and **Clare Island** are attractive islands with small *seabird* breeding populations. Clare Island is more accessible and now has the added attraction of Ireland's fourth *gannet* breeding station on an islet off the southern tip. The **Inishkea Islands** are two low-lying uninhabited islands off the Mullet peninsula. In winter they are the haunt of almost 2000 *barnacle geese,* the largest flock wintering in Ireland. This flock has been studied for over twenty years by Dr David Cabot of An Foras Forbartha. The island, however, is difficult of access and, frankly, *barnacle geese* are much more easily seen at a mainland site like Lissadell in County Sligo. A few kilometres north of the Inishkeas is **Inishglora** which holds a large *storm petrel* breeding population, many of the birds nesting among the boulders on a storm beach. Around the corner off the north coast are the virtually inaccessible **Stags of Broadhaven** where *Leach's petrels* have recently been proved to be still breeding. **Illaunmaister** off the north coast is an IWC reserve but is extremely hard to visit. Even to see the island requires a long walk from the nearest road on the mainland opposite the island. It holds breeding *puffins* and *storm petrels.*

The coastline from **Killary Harbour to Roonagh Quay** is sandy and has a string of small lakes, some holding nesting *terns.* Flocks of *sanderling* and *ringed*

MAYO

73

plovers winter at intervals all along the shore and overall numbers along the coast are quite high. Counts of similar areas in Scotland in recent years have disclosed very high populations: similarly thorough counts on the Connacht coast should also produce high totals.
Blacksod Bay is one of the few estuarine areas but the birds are almost unknown. There are a number of colonies of cliff-breeding birds on the north Mayo coast: my own favourite is **Downpatrick Head** because of its wildness and bleakness. *Fulmars* nest in abundance. Look out for the dark grey *blue fulmars*. I saw one on a nest site years ago on the stack at Downpatrick. Killala Bay holds wintering *ducks* and *waders* and the Moy estuary should be explored.

Much of north-west Mayo is bleak and relatively birdless blanket bog. The **Mullet** peninsula is wild and wind-blown with few trees, but in summer it holds breeding *corncrakes, dunlins, lapwings, snipe* and *redshanks*. In autumn *seabird* migration can be spectacular off **Annagh Head.** *Passerine* migrants can be interesting in autumn. Look out for *Lapland buntings* among the *finches.* **Termoncarragh Lake,** part of which is now an IWC reserve, is attractive for *waders* including North American vagrants.

Well inland are several great lakes. **Lough Conn** in north Mayo has thinly scattered winter populations of *ducks*, but has a notable breeding colony of *common scoters*. **Lough Cullen,** to the south of Lough Conn, has higher densities of diving *ducks* and there are indications that it may have large numbers of moulting *pochards* and *tufted ducks*. Farther south are **Loughs Carra** and **Mask.** Mask is a large, deep and disappointing lake for birds. Carra, however, is a wonderful *wildfowl* lake, shallow and, as the northern-most limestone lake, of interest for comparison with the Burren in County Clare. The flora is particularly interesting, but this lake also has the largest nesting *mallard* population in Ireland, a population which has been studied for many years. In winter, up to 2000 *mallard,* 500 *shovelers* and eighty-five *gadwall* can be seen. These lakes have important breeding concentrations of *seabirds* as well: *herring gulls, common gulls* and *common terns.*

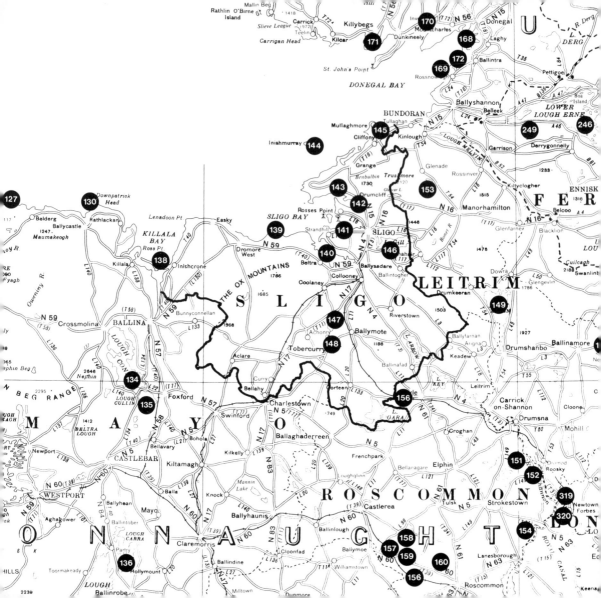

SLIGO

There has long been a group of dedicated naturalists resident in Sligo. The Sligo Field Club has been an active body for many years and, more recently, a branch of the Irish Wildbird Conservancy has been formed. There is very little published material on the birds, however, but an IWC leaflet entitled 'Where to watch birds in Sligo' compiled by Don Cotton should be read. This section relies heavily on it.

The Sligo coast is rich and varied. **Killala Bay,** already mentioned under County Mayo, should be visited as so little is known of it. From Killala to Ballysadare Bay the coast is rocky and has a fine cliff-breeding *seabird* colony at **Aughris Head.** Access must be made through pasture fields where no right of way exists, so permission should be sought from the farmer. *Fulmars, guillemots, razorbills* and *kittiwakes* nest here and some *seabird* movements can be seen offshore. This is one of the cliffs where counts are made every year as part of a scheme to monitor the breeding populations of Irish *seabirds*.

There are three broad bays readily accessible from Sligo town and each has its own distinctive avifauna. Unless you are very short of time, make sure to visit each of them. **Ballysadare Bay** is the most westerly and can be viewed from a number of points. The head of the estuary is muddy and holds *waders* and *wildfowl* including *mallard, teal* and *goldeneye.* Get to the shore via Ballysadare quarry to see the *waders* best. Streamstown off the main bay is a good area for *brent geese* and *shelduck* in winter. At the mouth of the bay *terns* roost on the sand bank in early autumn and in winter *red-breasted mergansers* can be seen.

The next bay, working eastwards, is **Cummeen Strand,** a vast area of inter-tidal sand which holds large numbers of

SLIGO

77

wigeons and *brent geese,* especially in October and November. *Gulls* roost where the Coney Island road meets the estuary: look out for *glaucous* and *Iceland gulls* here.

The final bay is **Drumcliff** which is best known among birdwatchers for the *barnacle goose* flock which winters at **Lissadell** on the northern shore. These are among the finest ornithological attractions in Ireland; most Irish wintering *barnacle geese* are on offshore islands and almost inaccessible. The Lissadell birds can be seen easily in a field between the road to Lissadell and the shore. Since the area was made a Forest and Wildlife Service sanctuary and the field fertilised the numbers of birds have increased substantially. A hide overlooking the field may be approached by entering the drive to Lissadell House and walking back in an easterly direction through the trees along the shoreline. It is easy to disturb the *geese* so approach carefully.

Inishmurray is a small and lovely island off the coast at Mullaghmore. Formerly with a human population, it is now an important breeding site for *eiders* and *storm petrels* with small numbers of *arctic* and *common terns.* In winter *barnacle geese* graze the island. **Bunduff Lake** is close to Mullaghmore and holds a small flock of *white-fronted geese.* Some *duck* species winter here in small numbers and *whooper swans* are invariable in winter.

Lough Gill was made famous by W.B. Yeats. The birdwatcher should visit the Hazelwood peninsula which projects out into the lake and has deciduous woodland with a good diversity of breeding *passerines.*

Templehouse Lake near Ballymote has good numbers of *ducks* and *whooper swans* with occasional *white-fronted geese.* The woodlands around the lake are good for *passerines.* **Doocastle Lake,** to the south of Templehouse, on the border with Mayo, holds similar species.

Barnacle geese

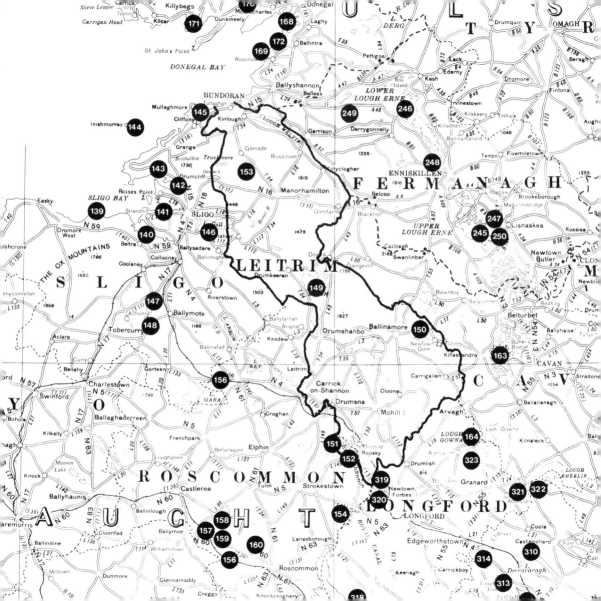

LEITRIM

This must be the county in Ireland which has been least watched by birdwatchers. Although it has a large number of lakes, very few of them have been visited regularly by any birdwatcher. We know that some areas have been known to hold interesting numbers of birds, but whether these are regular is not known.

Lough Allen appears to be rather disappointing for birds, presumably because of its depth and lack of shoreline. **Garadice Lough,** however, has some breeding and wintering *wildfowl*. On the Shannon the twin loughs of **Boderg** and **Bofin** have good numbers of *mallard* and *teal* together with small parties of *wigeon, goldeneye* and *tufted ducks,* and quite large numbers of wild *swans.* These lakes are difficult to get close to, however.

Leitrim should repay exploration in summer. *Great crested grebes* breed at a number of lakes and *garden warblers* on the rim of the lakes. **Glenade Lake** and the adjoining cliffs provide a wonderful breeding bird habitat and would repay further exploration.

LEITRIM

149. *Lough Allen*
150. *Garadice Lough*
151. *Lough Boderg*
152. *Lough Bofin*
153. *Glenade Lake*

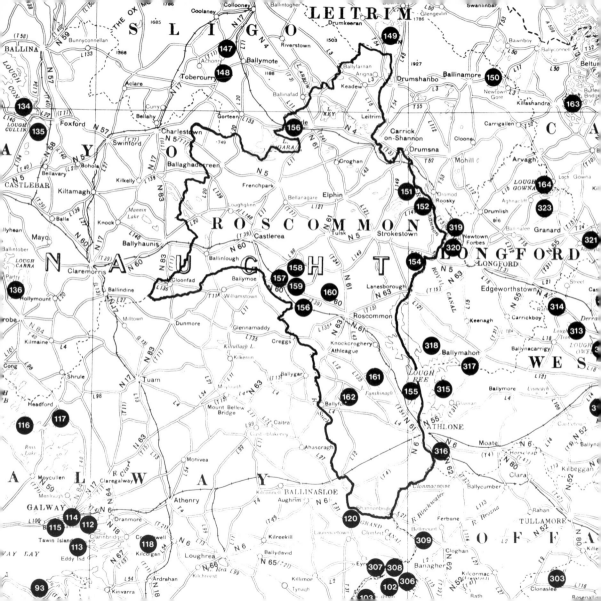

ROSCOMMON

Roscommon has few birdwatchers and there is little literature on the birds of the county. The principal geographical features of the county are the Shannon and its tributaries, and a large number of small lakes and turloughs. Many of these have large numbers of wintering *ducks* and *swans,* and some have important populations of breeding *ducks.*

The **River Shannon** between Athlone and Shannonbridge, as elsewhere, floods in winter and the callows hold *wigeon, teal, tufted ducks, pochard, mute swans, whooper swans* and *Bewick's swans.* In addition, there are large flocks of *lapwings* and *golden plovers,* and smaller numbers of *black-tailed godwits.* The **River Suck** is a major tributary of the Shannon and the upper stretch, between Ballyforan and Ballinasloe, has particularly valuable callows with exceptional numbers of *wigeon* and a small flock of *white-fronted geese.* Below Ballinasloe, there are still plenty of *ducks* and *swans,* but not quite so many as in the northern section.

Lough Ree is the second largest lake in the midlands but has relatively low numbers of wintering *wildfowl,* apart from *tufted ducks* which can be found in every bay. It is a fine place in summer, however, for breeding *ducks.*

A number of shallow lakes, some of them turloughs, provide fine bird habitats. These have the advantage of being much easier to watch than the broad and inaccessible Shannon. **Cloonlaughnan,** close to Mount Talbot, is a fine turlough with good numbers of *wigeon, teal, shoveler* and *pintail,* all of which can be seen easily. *Dunlins* and *black-tailed godwits* are also regular. **Briarfield, Castleplunket** and **Mullygollan** turloughs are all in the

ROSCOMMON

83

vicinity of Castleplunket and have *whooper* and *Bewick's swans* together with modest flocks of *ducks*. **Lisduff,** also known as Keenagh, is another turlough with similar birds. In autumn these turloughs must attract *ruffs, little stints, wood sandpipers* and other migrant *wader* species.

Permanent lakes like **Lough Funshinagh** and **Lough Croan** are better in summer than in winter. Both hold high concentrations of breeding *ducks* and *grebes* with a wide range of species present. Lough Funshinagh has a naturally fluctuating water level and extensive stands of clubrush and reeds. In winter it holds small numbers of *ducks* and *whooper swans,* and is occasionally used by the same *white-fronted goose* flock which frequents the River Suck. Approach from a minor road which runs past the south-east corner. Lough Croan is proably better nowadays, for both breeding and wintering *ducks*. The lake does dry out considerably in summer and is vulnerable to disturbance so do not walk the area during the breeding season.

Roscommon is a large county and has so much land under water that I have only been able to touch on the better-known places. Many others could prove most rewarding to the birdwatcher with some time to spend in the county.

ULSTER

Ulster comprises nine counties, six in Northern Ireland and three in the Republic, but the political boundary does not restrict birdwatchers who like to travel to see interesting birds. The province is dominated by Lough Neagh, the largest body of freshwater in Britain and Ireland and the winter haunt of enormous numbers of diving *ducks*. The northerly situation of the province means that some birds scarce elsewhere in Ireland, like *snow buntings, eiders* and, strangely, *buzzards*, are much more likely to be seen here than farther south. There are probably more birdwatchers in Ulster than in any other part of Ireland, mostly centred around Belfast and Derry, and the best bird areas are well known. The RSPB has published *Birds around Belfast*, an excellent booklet on the birds of the city and its environs, and *Birds beyond Belfast*, which lists the best birdwatching sites elsewhere in Northern Ireland. Both are essential reading for the visitor. The *Northern Ireland Bird Report* should be consulted for details of unusual species and *Birds of Northern Ireland* by C. Douglas Deane for an overall summary.

The three principal ornithological bodies operating in the province are the Donegal branch of the IWC, the Northern Ireland Ornithologists' Club and the RSPB. The last named has a number of reserves.

In this section I will first describe the birds of the counties in the Republic – Cavan, Monaghan and Donegal – and then deal with Northern Ireland, working from Derry east to Antrim, then south to Down and inland to Armagh, Tyrone and Fermanagh.

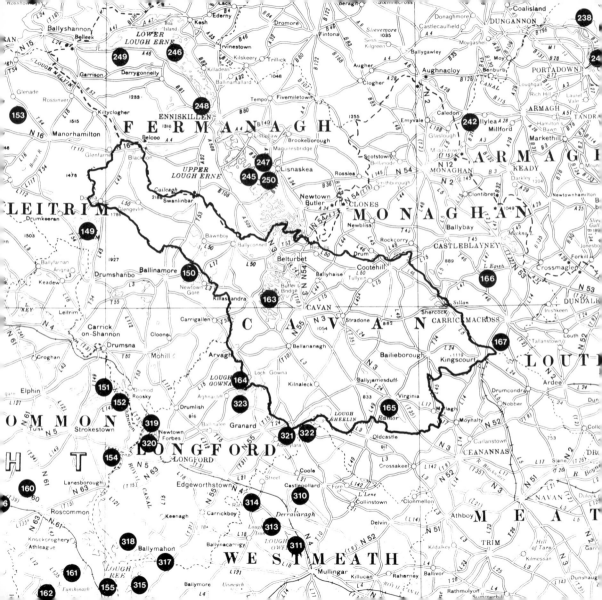

CAVAN

Cavan is a county of lakes and, unfortunately, few birdwatchers. Since it is far from Dublin, its birds are relatively little known. And, of course, it has no coastline.

Lough Oughter is the outstanding bird area, a very complex series of small and medium-sized lakes which has a sizeable population of breeding *tufted ducks* and *great crested grebes* in summer and, in winter, large numbers of diving *ducks, grebes* and, especially, *whooper swans*. It is still not known which are the best lakes for birds and the visitor would be well advised to move around the area, looking at as many lakes as possible, as there is always the possibility of an unusual *duck. Mallard, teal, shoveler* and *wigeon* should all be seen in winter, as should *tufted duck, pochard* and *goldeneye*. The woods hold *blackcaps* in summer.

Lough Gowna is another good *wildfowl* lake with similar species and, in summer, nesting *black-headed gulls, great crested grebes* and *ringed plovers*.

Lough Ramor in Virginia has smaller numbers of *ducks* and the Lough Sheelin shoreline has a good range of breeding birds including *lapwing, redshank, ringed plover, common sandpiper, coot, great crested grebe, tufted duck, grasshopper warbler* and *whinchat*.

CAVAN

163. *Lough Oughter*
164. *Lough Gowna*
165. *Lough Ramor*

87

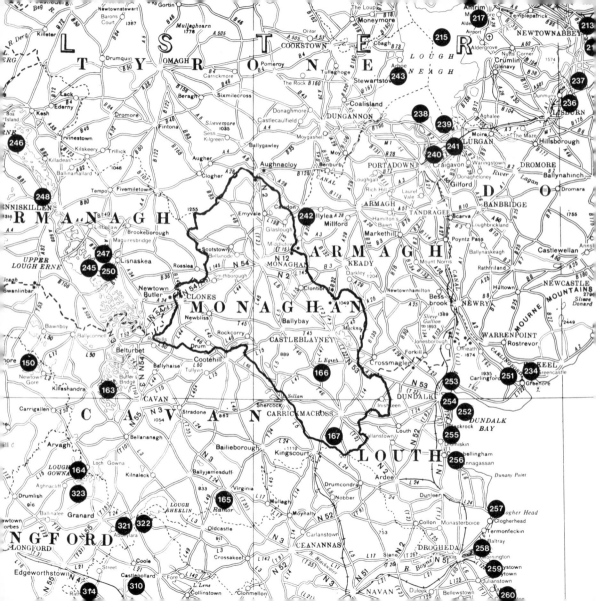

MONAGHAN

Another county with a number of lakes, which tend to be smaller than those in Cavan and less well known. Many of the lakes hold small populations of *duck* in winter and breeding *wildfowl* and *grebes* in summer. **Lough Egish** appears to be the best lake for birds with a large colony of breeding *gulls* and perhaps nesting *terns* as well. In winter it has *whooper* and *Bewick's swans* and a similar mix of *ducks* to the other midland lakes. For woodland birds the beechwoods at **Lough Fea Demesne,** some three kilometres south of Carrickmacross, should be visited. This area holds most of the common species and, in addition, has *jays* and *blackcaps,* which are less easy to see.

MONAGHAN

166. Lough Egish
167. Lough Fea Demesne

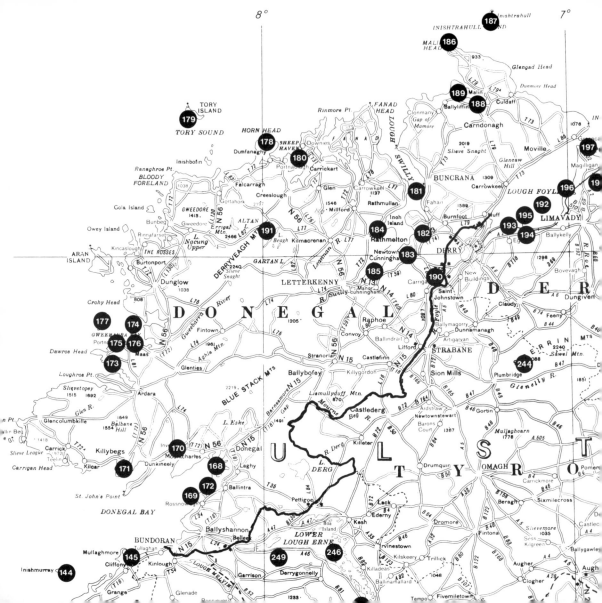

DONEGAL

The local branch of the IWC holds meetings in Letterkenny and Donegal town and its members were largely responsible for arranging the purchase by the IWC of its reserve at Sheskinmore Lough. There is currently no publication devoted solely to the birds of the county, but one is in preparation. The county has the only *red-throated divers* and *goosanders* nesting in Ireland and, because of its northerly location, is one of the most likely areas for colonisation by some of the species which have colonised Scotland in the past few decades as the climate has ameliorated. Much of the coast is ragged and fierce with deep inlets where *eiders* and some *long-tailed ducks* winter, but there are several bays where surface-feeding *ducks* and *waders* occur.

Donegal Bay is a large area where small numbers of *oystercatchers, curlews, redshanks* and *dunlin* can be seen on the shore and *common scoters* out to sea. In recent winters *surf scoters* from North America have been found among the *common scoters* off **Rossnowlagh.** All three species of *diver*, including regular *black-throated divers,* can be found at **Mountcharles.** At the westward end of the bay the fishing port of **Killybegs** attracts relatively large numbers of *glaucous* and *Iceland gulls.* **Birra Lough** near Rossnowlagh is worth a visit to see *whooper swans* and *ducks.* **Sheskinmore Lough** north of Ardara is an IWC reserve and one of the most important *white-fronted geese* haunts outside the Wexford slobs. It is one of the few places in Ireland where *white-fronted geese* and *barnacle geese* can be seen at the same site. In summer it holds a good concentration of breeding *waders* with at least six species recorded. A leaflet on the reserve is available from the IWC headquarters.

Gweebarra Bay, further north on the coast road, has similar birds to Donegal bay, including some *brent geese.* At the mouth of the bay *long-tailed ducks* winter in the sound, between **Portnoo** and **Inishkeel.** Out in the bay the island of **Roaninish** has a valuable colony of *storm petrels* which ringers from Copeland Bird Observatory in County Down have investigated in the past. *Barnacle geese*

DONEGAL

91

winter on the island but access is virtually impossible in winter. Drive on around the coast after looking at Roaninish and, if it is summer, take a trip to **Horn Head** where the largest colony of *razorbills* in Ireland breeds. The sheer cliffs are awesome and there has been understandable debate about the exact number of razorbills breeding on them. Out to sea **Tory Island** can be visited by mailboat. It was a bird observatory in the 1960s but has not been visited by ornithologists for many years. Difficulty of regular access was the principal reason for the abandonment of the observatory, but the migrants were interesting, especially late in autumn when *wildfowl*, *finches* and *thrushes* came in from the north.

West of Dunfanaghy is **Sheep Haven** which has not been the subject of much ornithological investigation. Mulroy Bay has been better watched but has relatively small numbers of *ducks* and *waders*.

The most interesting of the Donegal bays is **Lough Swilly,** which is also of course by far the largest of the bays. Much of it is deep and with little inter-tidal habitat, but the Inch Lough, Blanket Nook and Rathmelton are each rewarding places to visit. **Inch Lough** is the most spectacular in winter, a wonderful shallow lake with *whooper swans, Bewick's swans* and some *white-fronted geese*. Prior to the 1960s,

when it was partly drained, there were many more *geese*. Almost any species of *duck* may be come upon in winter and the place has the advantage of being easy of access by the main road to Inch Island. **Blanket Nook,** north of Newtown Cunningham, is smaller but has a similar variety of species and is probably better for *waders*. The inter-tidal zone near **Rathmelton** holds good numbers of *ducks* and *waders* but does not have the same diversity as Inch or Blanket Nook. It should, however, be visited.

Between Lough Swilly, the River Foyle and Lough Foyle is the best place in Ireland to see large numbers of wild *swans*. In winter 500–1400 *whooper* and several hundred *Bewick's swans* oscillate between a number of haunts in the area. The most important Donegal haunts are Inch, Blanket Nook and **Big Isle** near Manorcunningham. *White-fronted* and *greylag geese* occur in this area as well.

Malin Head, at the northerly tip of the Inishowen peninsula and **Inishtrahull,** an island north of Malin Head, were both migration watch-points in the 1960s and would reward visitors in September and October. Some remarkable sightings of northern birds arriving in Ireland were recorded.

Trawbrega Bay and the **Isle of Doagh** opposite Malin village are among the most rewarding places on the Inishowen peninsula. For a very full account of the entire area read Kenneth W. Perry's *The Birds of the Inishowen Peininsula* if you can get a copy of this 1975 publication. In summer *common, arctic* and *little terns* nest on the shingle beach on the west side of the Isle of Doagh. Offshore, *eiders* flock as they moult in late summer. *Lapwings* and *shelduck* nest in the meadows. In winter these same meadows hold *barnacle geese* and the mudflats of Trawbrega Bay have *brent geese, mallard, teal, wigeon* and *shoveler*. *Wader* numbers are small. Out in the bay *red-throated* and *great northern divers* are regular. Follow the road around the north shore and most of the birds can be observed with ease.

One other area where *wildfowl* and *waders* can be seen in numbers is the River Foyle between **Carrigans** and **Saint Johnstown,** upstream of Derry city.

This account of Donegal has been heavily biased towards the coast, but there is one outstanding inland site which every visitor to the county should get to during their stay. **Glenveagh National Park** is due south of Sheep Haven in north-west Donegal and surrounds Lough Veagh, a long narrow lake in the Derryveagh mountains. The park can be entered by turning south-west two-thirds of the way between Falcarragh and Kilcreenan. The estate is owned by the State and run by the Office of Public Works. Its principal

fame is as a haunt of red deer, but the combination of lake, mountain and woodland produces a fascinating mixture of bird communities. Montane birds such as *merlin, peregrine, red grouse, raven, golden plover* and *ring ouzel* occur with *willow warblers, skylarks, red-breasted mergansers* and even, at times, *goosanders*. A booklet on *Birds of Glenveagh* is available from the visitor centre at the entrance to the park. The park is nearly 1600 hectares in area so a great deal of time could be spent birdwatching here with value.

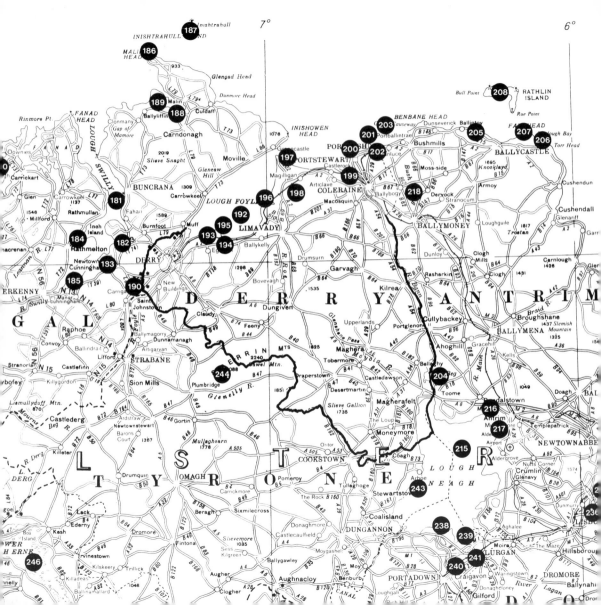

DERRY

There are several organisations in the county which encourage ornithology. The Ulster University Bird Club at Coleraine was a formidable body in the early 1970s but seems to have lapsed in recent years. Nowadays, the RSPB members' group at Limavady, the Route Naturalists' Field Club, the Limavady Field Club and the Londonderry Field Club hold outings and, as for many years, remain focal points for those interested in natural history in general.

Lough Foyle is a large open bay. At low tide the inter-tidal mudflats extend for up to two miles making observations difficult. When the tide rises, the large numbers of *wildfowl* and *waders* which use the areas retreat to roost on reclaimed land, shingle beaches and sand spits where they can be watched more easily. Work from Derry out towards Magilligan Point, watching out for *whooper swans, brent geese* (in autumn) and large flocks of *wigeon* and *waders*. There are a number of vantage points. Firstly, turn left from the main Limavady road at the White Horse Inn, fork right after 500 metres, fork left after another 800 metres, then continue on for another kilometre and a half to a level crossing where you can park. This is **Donnybrewer,** once a famous *goose* haunt, now much reduced in importance by drainage, but still holding good numbers of *duck*. **Eglinton Station** to the east (turn left off the main road, opposite the turn to Eglinton) is a good site for wild *geese* which gather on the reclaimed land. Return to the main road and get down to the mudflats at **Longfield** (past the Longfield Industrial Estate) where the largest flocks of *teal* and *wigeon* normally occur. The next good spot is the lagoon at Ballykelly (turn left at the crossroads in the village) where many *waders* roost at high tide. The **Roe estuary** can be reached with care, but a one-inch map is really essential to get to the south shore. The north shore is

95

accessible by turning left at a small garage just before Bellarena level crossing. *Bar-tailed godwits, curlews, redshanks* and other *waders* can be seen. Both the Roe estuary and Magilligan Point are national nature reserves and the foreshore between Longfield Point and the Roe estuary is an RSPB reserve with a warden who lives in Ballykelly.

Magilligan Point at the north-east corner of Lough Foyle is a good spot for looking for *snow buntings, great northern divers, red-throated divers* and *long-tailed ducks* in winter. In summer there is the possibility that *little terns* may nest. The Magilligan Field Centre should be visited and any interesting observations reported.

Gortmore viewpoint is a public carpark with a remarkable 250-metre high inland cliff face where *fulmars* breed in large numbers. It seems incongruous to find so many of these *seabirds* breeding inland, but of course it is not far to the shore. The carpark is well signposted from Downhill, mid-way between Magilligan and Coleraine. Look out for *buzzards* and *peregrines*.

The Bann estuary provides a greater possibility of seeing a rare bird than any of the Derry areas so far mentioned. A wide diversity of species has been recorded here in the past. Access is by left turn off the A2 at Articlave. Turn left

after a kilometre and a half at a T-junction, cross the bridge and turn right. Continue to the carpark. At a weekend you will almost certainly find other birdwatchers present.

Portstewart Point, just east of Portstewart Harbour, is a good seawatching site. *Eiders* are almost always present but watch out for *skuas;* almost any *seabird* is possible. The sewage outfall to the east of Portstewart provides an attraction for *kittiwakes* and, sometimes, *little gulls.* Look for *glaucous* and *Iceland gulls* in winter. **Ramore Head** at the end of the Portrush peninsula is another good seawatching place. There is a countryside centre on the coast at **Portrush** which provides information on all aspects of the natural history of the north coast. The **Skerries Islands** offshore hold wintering *barnacle geese* which can just be seen with a telescope.

The principal inland birdwatching spot in the county is **Lough Beg,** to the north of Lough Neagh (see below).

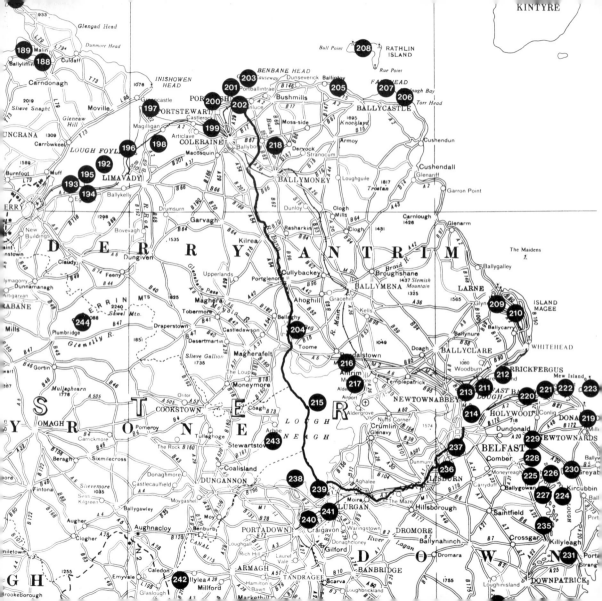

ANTRIM

The **North Antrim coast** is scenically very beautiful and, since much is owned by the National Trust for Northern Ireland, it can be walked. A long-distance footpath runs from the coast near Bushmills to Ballintoy Harbour and takes in the Giant's Causeway and Dunseverick Castle. The birds to watch for include *fulmars, gulls, black guillemots, eiders, turnstones, choughs* (beware cliff-nesting *jackdaws), buzzards, ravens* and *wheatears*.

Murlough Bay and **Fair Head** are also areas of outstanding natural beauty, though the birds to be seen are similar to those of much of the north coast. *Golden eagles* nested at Fair Head in the 1950s and hunted across the water in Scotland. *Buzzards* are regular here, so be careful in case you jump to the wrong conclusion about a large *bird of prey*. **Rathlin Island** offshore has a large *seabird* colony and a high density of breeding *buzzards*. The western tip at Kebble is the most interesting with offshore stacks crowded with *guillemots* and *kittiwakes*. There are two reserves here, a national nature reserve and an RSPB reserve, and a summer warden is employed from April to August. A booket *Birds of Rathlin Island* by Gerry Bond is available. Access is from Ballycastle by arrangement with local boatmen.

Larne Lough, close to Belfast, is an easily watched sea lough with saltmarsh and substantial mudflats. In winter *brent geese* and *whooper swans* are the most striking of the birds which occur but the common *grebes, wildfowl, waders* and *gulls* can all be seen. In summer **Swan Island** has breeding *terns*, including the rare *roseate terns*, and *red-breasted mergansers*. The island is an RSPB reserve and access is prohibited in summer.

On the **north shore of Belfast Lough** between Carrickfergus and Belfast there are several places on and just off the A2 where birds can be seen on the shore. The carparks a kilometre and a half south-west of **Carrickfergus** and at **Loughshore Park** near Jordanstown provide good vantage points, but a telescope is essential. *Oystercatchers, dunlin, curlews* and *redshanks* are the commoner *waders*. Many *gulls* occur; *glaucous, Iceland, little* and *Mediterranean* should be sought. *Grebes* offshore and *seaducks* can be seen at Carrickfergus. *Eiders, long-tailed ducks* and *common scoter* are usually present off the harbour entrance. **Duncrue Street Marsh,** three kilometres from the centre of Belfast, has freshwater lagoons which attract a number of *wader* species not usually seen on the adjoining mudflats of the Lough. Drive north from Belfast for the M2, turning right for Duncrue Street. Follow Duncrue Street on to Duncrue Road, then park your car and walk along the

ANTRIM

cattle path. The marsh is an excellent place in autumn for passage *waders* such as *ruffs, little stints* and *curlew sandpipers*. It is probably the best Northern Ireland site for American *waders*. On the left hand side of the path the Herdman Channel has good numbers of *waders*. North of the marsh is a rubbish tip where *glaucous* and *Iceland gulls* can frequently be found. *Short-eared owls* are regular in winter. Duncrue Street is at its best in autumn.

Inland in County Antrim the most outstanding place for birds is the Lough Beg/Lough Neagh complex. **Lough Beg**, to the north of Lough Neagh, has been written about by Gordon D'Arcy in *Birds at Lough Beg*, a beautifully illustrated book published by Blackstaff Press. Lough Beg is a shallow lake just north of Toome where the River Bann broadens out for about five kilometres. Gordon D'Arcy lists 171 species which had been recorded up to the end of 1976 and includes such rarities as *white stork, red-crested pochard, goshawk* and *greater yellowlegs*. In winter thousands of diving *ducks* and hundreds of wild *swans* assemble and this is one of the best times to visit the area. But it is an exciting place at all seasons; in summer *lapwings, redshanks, snipe* and *curlew* breed in fair numbers with smaller numbers of *dunlin* and *ringed plovers*.

Lough Beg is an extension of **Lough Neagh,** which is by far the largest lake in Ireland. Large flocks of diving *ducks* can be seen around much of the shoreline. Indeed, counts of over 30,000 each of *tufted duck* and *pochard* have been made by the Northern Ireland Ornithologists' Club. All the other common species occur in winter, and some of the rare species (*goosander, smew, red-crested pochard, ferruginous duck*) are more likely to turn up somewhere on this shoreline than elsewhere in Ireland. **Shane's Castle,** an RSPB reserve on the north shore of the lough, is only twenty-nine kilometres from Belfast and probably the best place to see a representative sample of the birds of Lough Neagh. Take the M2 from Belfast, leaving the motorway at the sign for Ballymena and Coleraine. Turn left on the first road at the roundabout and follow the signposts for Shane's Castle. The reserve is a popular place for outings because of its attractive woodland, its steam railway and the old ruined castle, as well as its birds. The castle provides an excellent vantage point for scanning the lough with a telescope. Flocks of *pochard* and *tufted ducks* with smaller numbers of *teal, gadwall, mallard, scaup, goldeneye* and *whooper* and *Bewick's swans* can all be seen in winter. In summer *little grebes, great crested grebes, tufted ducks* and *common terns* nest in the reserve. The woodland area is good for small birds. Use the nature trail. In summer *blackcaps* and *woodcock* nest but all the common woodland birds breed as well. Rare birds have been seen and you should keep an eye open for mammals (fallow deer, badgers, otters and pine martens).

Rea's Wood, behind the Deer Park Hotel about three kilometres south of Shane's Castle, is another attractive woodland area with good viewing conditions for the *wildfowl* of Lough Neagh. Further north in Antrim is **Garry Bog,** a large bog eight kilometres north of Ballymoney, where wild *swans* can be seen in winter. In summer *grasshopper warblers* can be heard.

There are, of course, a number of other woodland and scrub areas and small loughs where small birds can be seen and readers are urged to explore their own localities.

Bramblings

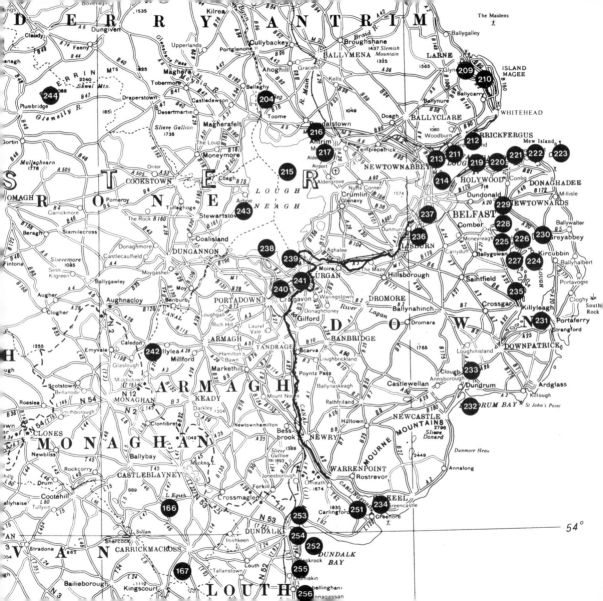

DOWN

Birdwatching in Down is dominated by the opportunities presented on the south shore of Belfast Lough and in Strangford Lough. The county is one of the best watched in Ireland but the discovery in recent years of several rare *gulls* at the little fishing port of Portavogie illustrates the value of regularly watching one's local area rather than rushing around the country looking at the better known places. As with County Antrim the best guide is the excellent *Birds around Belfast* published by the Belfast RSPB members' group.

Kinnegar on the south shore of Belfast Lough is approached from Holywood, five kilometres north-east of Belfast. Turn left at the Esplanade in Holywood, drive under the railway and turn left. Drive to the army depot and turn right. Park there and walk along the shore. Within a couple of hours of high tide *waders* can be seen in good numbers and *great crested grebes, shelduck, goldeneye, wigeon* and *eiders* can also be watched in winter. *Shelduck, mallard, lapwings* and *black-headed gulls* breed in the marshy areas of Belfast Harbour Airport grounds and can be seen at a distance, but entrance to the grounds is prohibited.

From **Holywood to Bangor** a footpath runs beside the shore for about sixteen kilometres. *Cormorants, shags, red-breasted mergansers, eiders* and, in winter, *great crested grebes* can usually be seen. On the shore look out for *purple sandpipers* among the *turnstones*. **Bangor sea front** is famed for its *black guillemots* which nest in holes in the pier and can be seen at extremely close range. The common species of *gull* occur and *glaucous gulls* are fairly frequent. In recent years both *Bonaparte's* and *ivory gulls* have been seen here.

Groomsport is a village three kilometres beyond Bangor and has breeding *arctic terns* in the harbour. The **Copeland Islands** are a group of three small islands which can be reached from Donaghadee.

DOWN

103

One has been a bird observatory for nearly thirty years. Manning is regular at weekends in spring and autumn and the regulars have carried out a study of *Manx shearwaters* over many years. The observatory members organise other activities when off the island; these include expeditions to other islands and ringing on the Down mainland.

Strangford Lough is a huge sealough with very large numbers of wintering *wildfowl* and *waders*. Much of the foreshore is controlled by the National Trust for Northern Ireland under its Strangford Lough Wildlife Scheme and there are several national nature reserves within the Lough. In autumn the Lough can hold over 15,000 *brent geese* and 10,000 *wigeon*, but the area is so great that it would take weeks to thoroughly explore the shoreline. Fortunately for Belfast residents, who live only twenty kilometres away, the largest numbers of birds occur at the northern end where the RSPB members' group recommends six access points.

Castle Espie is three kilometres south-east of Comber and an excellent place from mid-September for *brent geese* and *wigeon*. The common *waders* also occur and there is a private *wildfowl* collection on the brackish lagoon beside the carpark, where there is also an excellent National Trust hide. Look out in autumn for *ruffs*, *black terns* and other passage migrants.

Reagh Island is reached by continuing south towards Mahee Island from Castle Espie. There is a small carpark on the left, one kilometre after the right turn at a causeway. The diversity of birds is less than at Castle Espie but *greylag geese*, *pintail* and *black-tailed godwits* are usually to be seen in autumn and winter.

Whiterock is easily found by following the signposts from Comber via Ardmillan and is a sailing centre, but also quite good for birds.

Island Hill, four kilometres north-east of Comber, and just off the road to Newtownards is an excellent place for seeing *brent geese*. *Grey plovers* and *greenshanks* are usually present, apart from in summer, and so are the more common *waders*. *Tree sparrows* occur here.

The Maltings is two kilometres south of Newtownards, is an excellent place for Lough and has similar birds to the other sites mentioned though *whooper swans* and *pintail* are noteworthy.

Greyabbey is a small village eleven kilometres south-east of Newtownards where *brent geese* can usually be seen. In several recent years one or two *black brant*, the North American race of the *brent*, have been seen among the *geese*. The area also has a freshwater lough and *pochard*, *tufted ducks* and *goldeneye* are present in winter.

At the south end of Strangford Lough large numbers of *Sandwich, common, arctic* and even some *roseate terns* nest on the islands, but access is limited during the breeding season. At **Castleward** near Strangford village is a *wildfowl* collection where many of the species which occur on the Lough can be seen. The collection is run by the National Trust and is open to the public.

Dundrum Bay stretches from St John's Point, a good seawatching spot, in the east to Newcastle in the west. Most of it is sandy beach but there is a small tidal inlet with mudflats at **Inner Dundrum Bay**. The sand dunes at Murlough National Nature Reserve on the west side of the bay are owned by the National Trust, whose wardens are the best source of information on how to spend a day birdwatching in the area.

There are wintering *teal, mallard* and *wigeon* in the inner bay and large flocks of *common scoter* in the outer bay. Look out for *velvet scoters*, even *surf scoters* from North America, among the *common scoters*. There is a countryside centre on the promenade in nearby Newcastle where information on the natural history of the Mourne Mountains region may be obtained.

Carlingford Lough north shore has *brent geese* and is notable for its flock of *scaup* which can be seen farther out in the bay.

Inland there are a number of estates where woodland birds can be seen and several particularly interesting spots. **Clea Lakes** are three kilometres from Killyleagh on the south-west side of Strangford and have nesting *great crested grebes, mallard* and *tufted ducks*. The **Lagan Towpath** which runs for sixteen kilometres from the Stranmillis Embankment of the Lagan in Belfast to the Hillsborough Road Bridge outside Lisburn has a variety of freshwater habitats: river, stream, abandoned canal, pasture and hedgerow. The birds have been well studied and the area is known as excellent in both summer and winter for *little grebes, water rails, moorhens, kingfishers, dippers* and many *passerines*.

Belvoir Park Forest on the southern side of Belfast has had thirty-five species recorded breeding including *blackcap, chiffchaff, sparrowhawk* and *jay*. The Northern Ireland office of the RSPB is located on the estate.

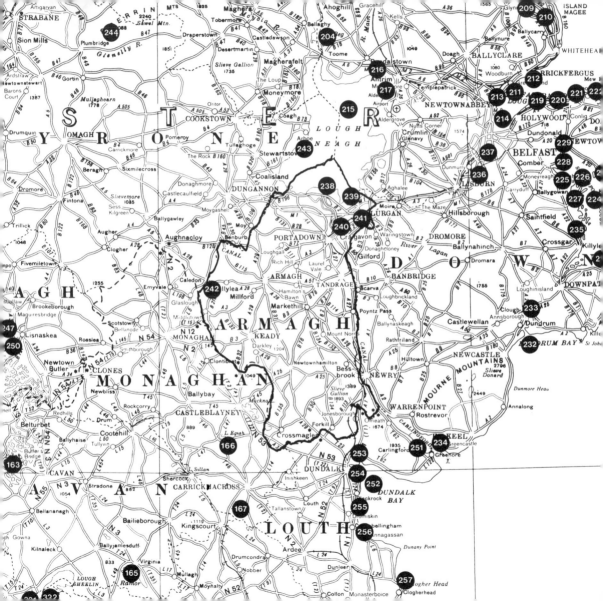

ARMAGH

The **south shore of Lough Neagh** is the principal birdwatching place in the county. The **Oxford Island Nature Reserve** on Lough Neagh, **Craigavon Lake** and **Lurgan Park Lake** hold a population of diving *ducks* which move around between each area. There is a high density of breeding *great crested grebes* at Oxford Island and the reserve has a visitor centre and hide. Several pairs of *corncrakes* still breed in the area. This is perhaps the best part of the Lough Neagh basin for rare diving *ducks*: *ring-necked ducks, smew, red-crested pochard* and *ferruginous ducks* have all been seen in recent years. The entire shoreline is good for *wildfowl* and the road runs along much of the edge of the Lough.

Up to a hundred *Greenland white-fronted geese* frequent the **Annaghroe** area beside the Blackwater river about two kilometres south-west of Caledon. Take the A28 from Caledon for Aughnacloy; after a kilometre turn left onto the B45. Continue on this road for about a kilometre until you reach a large area of open grassland on your right. Scan from the road for *geese* and *whooper swans* in winter and, in spring, *golden plover*.

Inland, Armagh is generally low-lying with slow streams and some estates scattered through the farmland. *Grasshopper warblers* and *blackcaps* can be found nesting.

ARMAGH

107

TYRONE

Tyrone is a large county bordering the **western shore of Lough Neagh** between the Blackwater and Ballinderry rivers. The west and south-west sides of Lough Neagh generally have the largest rafts of *pochard* and *tufted ducks*, and a scattering of *whooper* and *Bewick's swans* in winter. In summer large numbers of *black-headed gulls* nest on the islands along the shore.

To the west the **Sperrin Mountains** still hold breeding *golden plover*, albeit at low density. *Peregrines*, *ravens* and *red grouse* also occur. There is a good population of *hen harriers* in the county and *siskins* and *crossbills* can be found in a number of the upland plantations such as Lough Bradan Forest.

FERMANAGH

Perhaps the most underrated part of Ulster for birdwatching, Fermanagh is divided in two by **Lough Erne**. The **Upper Lough** holds large numbers of breeding *great crested grebes* and a very large *heronry* on one of the islands. The **Lower Lough**, dotted with many islands, is even richer in breeding birds. The highlight is the *common scoter* breeding population of approximately fifty pairs. The RSPB has a reserve at Castle Caldwell at the western end of the Lough where *common scoters* and *great crested grebes* can be seen with ease. You never know what may turn up. Recently, one visitor to the Lough found a male *surf scoter* (an American species) and a male *velvet scoter* among the summering *common scoters*. There was, unfortunately, no sign of a female for either. *Black terns* were proved to nest in the past. *Common* and *Sandwich terns* nest regularly.

The numerous lakes around Upper Lough Erne deserve exploring. The whole area is very important for *whooper swans*: large flocks regularly winter beside **Murlough Lake** north of Newtown Butler and are easily visible from the road. The mouth of the **Colebrook River** west of Lisnaskea also has large numbers.

The county has many wooded areas where *jays*, *blackcaps* and other woodland birds nest. **Lough Navan Forest** has

TYRONE

243. Western shore
of Lough Neagh
244. Sperrin Mountains

FERMANAGH

245. Upper Lough Erne
246. Lower Lough Erne
247. Murlough Lake
248. Colebrook River
249. Lough Navan Forest
250. Drumgay Lough

Grey heron

breeding *crossbills* and observers should look out for *hen harriers, peregrines* and *red grouse*. Small parties of *Greenland white-fronted geese* frequent the area in winter. The forest has numerous roads through it and is well signposted off the main Enniskillen – Belleek road (A45) near Derrygonnelly. **Drumgay Lough**, five kilometres north of Enniskillen, is a bird sanctuary and has a good selection of *wildfowl*.

LEINSTER

Leinster has the largest city in Ireland at
its hub and consequently its birds are
relatively well known. There is much less
chance of coming on a very good and
still unknown place for birds than there
is in the other provinces. Nevertheless,
parts of the midland counties, well
within reach of Dublin, are not all that
well known. My tour of the counties will
work from north to south along the coast
and then move inland: Louth, Meath,
Dublin, Wicklow, Wexford, Kilkenny,
Carlow, Laois, Kildare, Offaly,
Westmeath and Longford.

LOUTH

A number of Dublin birdwatchers developed a keen interest in the birds of Louth in the early 1970s and a *Louth Bird Report* was edited by Colm Moore for a couple of years. Unfortunately, this died and a lot of material on the birds remained in birdwatchers' notebooks for some years until 1980 when the annual *Irish East Coast Bird Report* was established to cover Louth, Meath, Dublin and Wicklow. This is essential reading for those seriously interested in the birds of Louth.

Carlingford Lough marks the border between Northern Ireland and the Republic. A large flock of *scaup* which feed in the lough are the most unusual feature, but the habitat is ideal for *grebes* and *divers* as well as the *ducks* and *waders* which are typical of most of the Leinster estuaries. A small flock of *brent geese* winters here. From Greenore to Omeath the road runs close to the sea and provides a number of vantage points.

Dundalk Bay has had more *waders* counted on it than any Irish estuary apart from the much larger Shannon estuary and Strangford Lough. The area is really not an estuary, though several rivers do flow into the bay; in fact it is a huge, broad, sandy bay with several saltmarsh areas where birds concentrate at high tide. The sand harbours cockles, the food of the *oystercatchers* and

oystercatchers are among the most obvious birds here.

Working from the north, drive out to Giles' Quay on the Carlingford peninsula and then work back to **Ballymascanlan Bay**. Make sure you look out to sea for *grebes* or diving *ducks*. If the tide is high, *waders* roost on the shore beside the main road; if low, the sand will be dotted with birds. Watch for some *black-tailed godwits* in the muddy estuary at Ballymascanlan; the *bar-tailed godwit* is, however, the common species here and several thousand winter in the bay. The **South Marsh** is one of the two largest roosts in the area. Drive east from Dundalk to Soldier's Point and walk the marsh from here if the tide is high. Take great care, however, as the channels are deep and many are impassable. Most of the *waders* roost on islands which can only be reached by boat. If you are working the area thoroughly you will need to walk most of the marsh; if not, then drive towards Blackrock and stop where the road meets the sea. Look back across the marsh, particularly if the tide has started to ebb, for a sight of masses of birds moving out of the vegetation and onto the sand.

Lurgangreen is the other enormous roost. Like the South Marsh, this is an extensive area of saltmarsh and it can be approached easily by taking the first left turn on the main Belfast–Dublin road

LOUTH

113

after you join it from Blackrock. Look for the bridge over the Fane River and turn left immediately afterwards. The lane brings you down to the shore. Walk south to the sea-wall and then walk as far south as you can behind the cover of the sea-wall, emerging slowly and cautiously to watch the wheeling flocks of *waders*. Thousands of *golden plover*, *dunlin*, *knot*, *oystercatchers* and *lapwing* roost here and smaller numbers of other species. Almost any species of *duck* can be seen and *greylag*, *brent*, *barnacle* and *white-fronted geese* all occur occasionally.

Further south, large numbers of *waders* roost on the beach near the mill at **Annagassan** where they can be easily seen.

Clogher Head protrudes relatively far out into the Irish Sea and was watched intensively for a few years in the mid-1970s. The large *scoter* flock was found to contain some *velvet scoters* and, indeed, the occasional *surf scoter* from North America. In autumn, *seabird* passage, especially movement of *skuas*, was interesting (up to 280 *arctic skuas* in an autumn) and some scarce *passerine* migrants were recorded on the head and in the few gardens nearby. The highlight of watching at Clogher Head was Ireland's first *rock thrush* in May 1974, proving that exotic birds can appear at the most unexpected places. *Glaucous gulls* are almost always present at the head and *Mediterranean gulls* are occasional.

The **Boyne estuary**, from Drogheda to the sea, is an easily watched estuary but one which requires a thorough search as birds can very easily be missed. On the north side the road runs from Drogheda to Baltray and the area from Queensborough to Baltray tends to hold most of the *ducks*, mainly *wigeon*, and many of the *waders*. On the southern shore, the road to Mornington provides easy access to the mudflats where most of the *black-tailed godwits* feed. Good views can be obtained of them here.

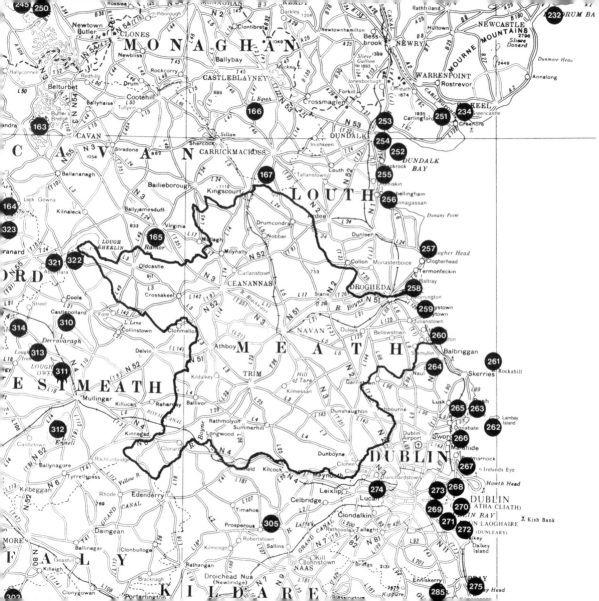

MEATH

Although the area of the county is large there are no known bird haunts of any importance in Meath, apart from the estuary of the River Nanny at **Laytown** which holds some *ducks* and *waders*. Offshore, search for *common scoters* and perhaps *velvet scoters*, especially in November, at Laytown or **Gormanston**.

The literature on the birds is restricted to the *Irish East Coast Bird Report* published annually since 1980.

MEATH

259. *Laytown*
260. *Gormanston*

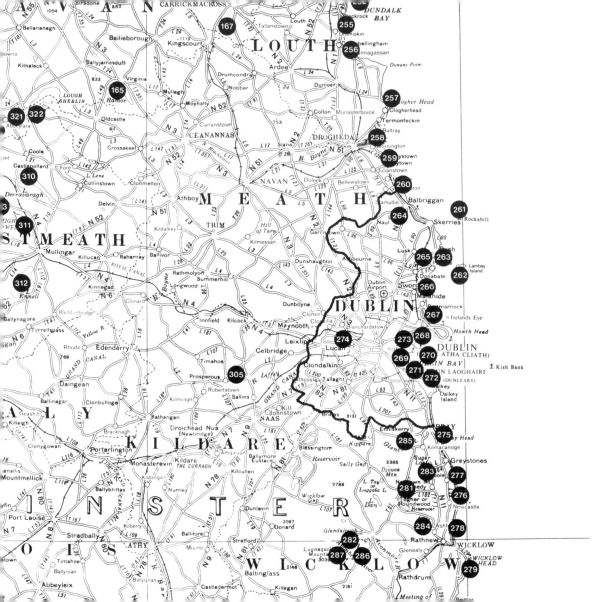

DUBLIN

The birds of County Dublin are probably the most written about and most closely watched in the country. The county is quite small but its coastline has several fine estuaries with large numbers of *wildfowl*. The coast also has sea-cliffs and islands with nesting *seabirds*. Inland there is excellent variety of habitat from woodland to mountain. The first book published on the birds of Dublin was by Rev. P.G. Kennedy SJ, *An Irish Sanctuary — the Birds of the North Bull*. Father Kennedy was primarily responsible for educating Dubliners in the birds of their city and his book, though published in 1953, is still a lovely evocation of the birds of the Bull. More recently, my own *The Birds of Dublin and Wicklow* published in 1975 contains an account of the birds of both counties, and *North Bull Island, Dublin Bay — a Modern Coastal Natural History*, edited by David Jeffrey, and published in 1977, contains expert accounts of all aspects of the natural history of the North Bull. Since 1980 the county's bird records have been published in the annual *Irish East Coast Bird Report*. There are four IWC branches, covering northside, central and southside Dublin and Fingal.

Rockabill island off the north Dublin coast is an old established *tern* colony but is not really approachable. It is now the largest surviving colony of *roseate terns* in Ireland.

Lambay Island lies south of Rockabill and is a much larger island owned by Lord Revelstoke and inhabited by a small human population. The island may not be landed on without permission from the owner, but it is the largest *seabird* colony on the east coast between Rathlin and Saltee and in winter holds a small flock of *barnacle geese* and, occasionally, *greylag geese*. With a good telescope the *geese* can be seen, though not specifically identified, from the mainland.

Rush and the surrounding lands hold *tree sparrows* and large numbers of *finches* in winter. **Knock Lake**, off the main Dublin – Belfast road near Naul, holds diving *ducks* and occasionally a rarity. *Ring-necked duck* and *goosander* have both been seen.

Rogerstown estuary is one of the country's most important wetlands holding large flocks of *shelduck, brent geese, wigeon* and *teal* with smaller numbers of *pintail* and *shoveler*. The surrounding fields held *greylag geese* in the 1940s and early 1950s, but these departed because of changes in land use and the erection of greenhouses. *Wader* numbers are high and the estuary

DUBLIN

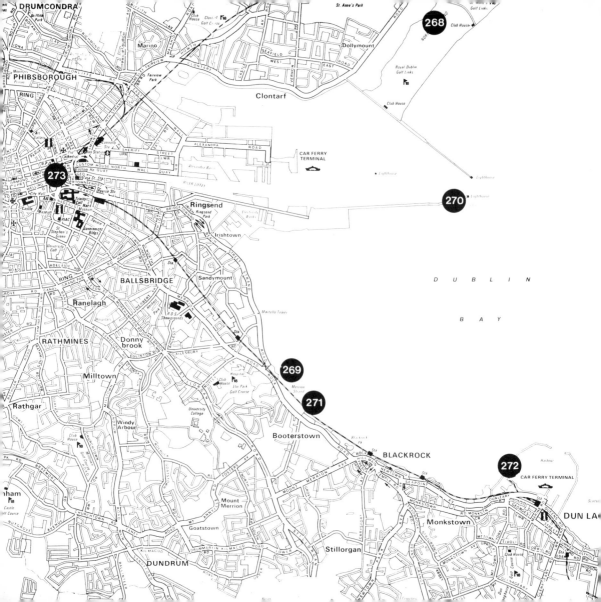

regularly holds scarce species in autumn like *little stints, curlew sandpipers* and *ruffs.* Unfortunately, Dublin County Council has taken the view that the estuary, being devoid of surrounding housing estates, is a suitable case for large-scale dumping of domestic refuse. Whether any estuary will remain here in twenty years is a moot point: posterity will deal harshly with the reputations of those who took the decisions which led to the destruction of this habitat.

The best way to work the area is to turn right off the main Dublin–Belfast road about five kilometres north of Swords where the North Dublin Growers Co-op warehouse stands. Turn right when coming from Dublin and turn right again at the fork a kilometre on. Go to the tiphead and explore the western end of the estuary. This is much the best place and both the pools behind the estuary and the open mudflat should be watched carefully. Look out for rare *gulls* at the tiphead and keep an eye open for *snow buntings* or *Lapland buntings.* Along the river from the saltmarsh back to Newhaggard Bridge is one of the best Irish sites for *green sandpipers.*

If you have travelled by car, after working the estuary above the railway causeway, travel to the little pier at the mouth of the estuary. The seaward side of the causeway is usually less productive than the section above it.

The birds on the north Dublin estuaries move about from bay to bay. **Malahide** estuary is very similar to Rogerstown on the seaward side of the railway causeway. The species you see are similar, though numbers are smaller. Above the causeway, at Broadmeadows, is a sheltered water popular for sailing and water-skiing. This is a good place for seeing *great crested grebes, red-breasted mergansers, goldeneyes* and a few *scaup* and *long-tailed ducks,* though a telescope is usually necessary in addition to binoculars if all the birds are to be identified. At the Swords end of the estuary, just below Lissenhall Bridge, is an area of grassy islands where *waders* can be seen at close range. The variety of species is surprising. *Curlew sandpipers* are regular in autumn and *spotted redshanks* and *ruffs* are frequent. As the water-level above the railway bridge has a tidal rhythm of only a few centimetres the mudflat here is almost always exposed. So the area provides a fine roost-site for birds which feed at low-tide on the seaward side of the estuary.

This is an attractive estuary to visit with a variety of habitat. Cover the grassy islands, the open water at Broadmeadows, the estuary between Donabate and the causeway and look at the open sea as well.

Baldoyle estuary has the lowest number of birds of any of the north Dublin estuaries, largely because large sections have been overgrown with *Spartina* grass. *Brent geese* and *wigeon* both feed here. Sometimes a *slavonian grebe* or two may be seen at the southern end of the estuary.

The **North Bull**, which lies just south of Baldoyle, is the jewel for Dublin birdwatchers. Running almost the length of the north side of Dublin bay it includes a variety of habitats, all of which are worth visiting. The visitor who just wants good views of *ducks* and *geese* should visit the Bull at low tide. Start at Fairview and walk the length of the road to Sutton. Far better views will be obtained than from the saltmarsh on the island because the birds are accustomed to passing traffic on the road, whereas walkers on the saltmarsh cause disturbance. At Fairview look out for diving *ducks* like *goldeneye* and *red-breasted mergansers*. Several hundred *brent geese* may be seen especially in late winter grazing on park grassland just east of the Fairview railway bridge. Watch the *waders* on the mudflat on this stretch: *black-tailed godwits* can usually be found. Flocks of *teal* and *wigeon* are found from the bridge across to the island onwards, with the very largest *duck* flocks concentrated close to the causeway and on both sides. The flock which gathers around the outlet from the freshwater stream in St Anne's Estate is normally particularly close to the road and

contains *wigeon, teal, mallard, pintail* and *shoveler*. Rarer ducks have occurred: the most spectacular I recall was a vivid male *blue-winged teal* from North America which became famous after appearing on television.

Do not feel that you have seen it all by the time you reach the causeway because the mix of species from here to Sutton is different. Diving *ducks* reappear and large numbers of *brent geese* and *shelduck* feed on the *Zostera* (eel-grass) and on *Hydrobia* (small snails) respectively. Stop and contemplate the vast productivity required from the mudflats to support the 6000 *wildfowl* and 25,000 *waders* which feed along the Bull channel. If you are interested in the topic, buy the marvellous book edited by Dr David Jeffrey (see p. 119).

It really requires most of a day to thoroughly work the North Bull from the mainland. Another day is needed to work the area from the island side. If you want to count the birds, the best technique is to walk the saltmarsh just after high tide when most of the birds which spread out across Dublin Bay to feed at low water are roosting on the Bull. Walk around the flocks trying not to disturb them. Counts of 10,000 *knot*, 9900 *dunlin*, 5000 *oystercatchers* and 2500 *bar-tailed godwits* have been made on the Bull: a team of counters is really necessary for the best results. *Short-eared owls* normally hunt the saltmarsh in winter and a *peregrine* is frequently present. Visit the little alder marsh in autumn and look for migrants. *Redstarts* and *whinchats* have been seen there.

The Bull is only part of the Dublin Bay area, albeit the best part. On the southern side of the Liffey, **Sandymount strand** from the South Wall south to Booterstown is another excellent birdwatching area. Drive out along the South Wall to the ESB power station and walk from there to the **Poolbeg lighthouse.** *Purple sandpipers* feed around the sea-wall with *turnstones*; in summer and autumn the area is popular among *terns* as a rich fishing ground. From the South Wall across to Dún Laoghaire lie scattered parties of sea *ducks*, mostly *common scoter. Great crested grebes* and *divers* also occur here. Sandymount strand is so large that it is not feasible to watch all the birds at low tide. When the tide is nearly full or just starting to ebb are the best times. Flocks of *gulls* can be very large and in recent years *Mediterranean gulls* have been regular and *glaucous, Iceland* and *ring-billed* occurred occasionally. In August an enormous flock of thousands of *terns*, including many *roseate terns*, comes in to roost each evening. In early winter *brent geese* may be seen close to the railway crossing at Merrion gates.

Booterstown marsh, south of Merrion gates, is a small marsh where *teal, lapwing, redshanks* and other *waders* can be seen at close range.

The **West Pier, Dún Laoghaire,** is a traditional birdwatching spot. Over twenty years ago daily migration watches were carried out here every morning in spring and autumn and the results correlated with observations at more obvious bird observatories such as Great Saltee in County Wexford and Bardsey in Wales. Numbers of birds were lower as one would expect but 'falls' of migrants were reflected at the West Pier just as at other watch-points. Nowadays the pier is best known as a location for scanning Dublin Bay for *common scoters, long-tailed ducks* and *divers*. At times, *long-tailed ducks* and *red-throated divers* come right in to the sea-wall. Rarities such as *black-throated diver, red-necked grebe* and *velvet scoter* have occurred.

Dublin City has several good birdwatching sites. **O'Connell Street** in the centre of the city has a large and long-established roost of *pied wagtails* in the trees in the middle of the street. The **Phoenix Park** is a wonderful recreation area with populations of woodland birds which can be seen easily and, of course, Dublin Zoo. The Zoo is worth visiting for close views of the *ducks* and *geese* which can be difficult to approach in the wild.

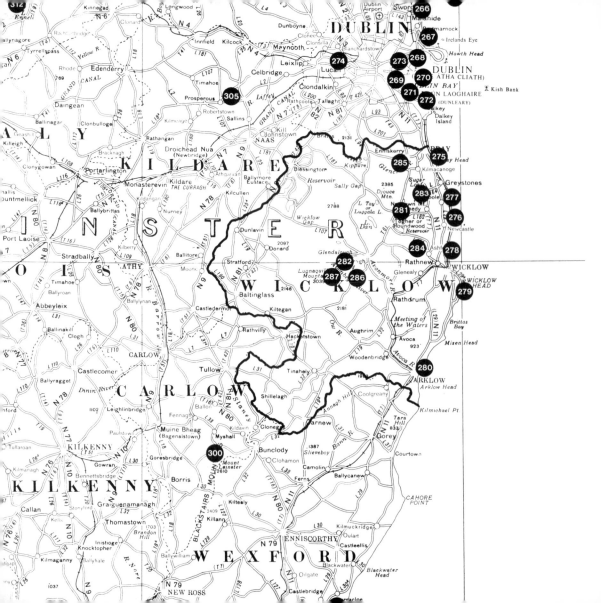

WICKLOW

Because it is so accessible to Dublin dwellers, north Wicklow has been almost as well watched as Dublin, but south Wicklow is much less well known. The county's most notable features for the birdwatcher are its breeding raptors and its woodland birds, but it also has some interesting coastal sites. The standard work on the birds of the county is my own *The Birds of Dublin and Wicklow* published by the Irish Wildbird Conservancy in 1975 and the county is covered nowadays by the *Irish East Coast Bird Report*. There is an active IWC branch in the county.

Bray Head holds a growing colony of nesting *gulls* and is an excellent place to see *black guillemots*. They can usually be seen from the train which runs around the head. *Manx shearwaters* almost certainly nest here still, though in small numbers. If you want to check this, be prepared for hard work as the *shearwaters* nest in burrows above the cliff, only coming ashore or emerging from the burrows at night.

The stretch of coastline from **Greystones to Wicklow** town provides an invigorating walk past a variety of pools, reed-beds and pasture which hold small numbers of birds but usually include species which are difficult to see elsewhere. In late winter *little gulls* can be seen along this coast dipping down into the breaking surf for food. Once extremely rare they are now regular along this stretch of shoreline and flocks of over a hundred have been seen. Walk along the strand and beside the railway line. If you are visiting the area in spring or autumn watch for migrants in the scrub. About half a kilometre south of the old **Kilcoole** railway station you will see a large, muddy tidal pool on your right. This floods in stormy weather and forms a large lake. Within days of flooding *Bewick's swans,* and occasionally *whooper swans,* appear. Small numbers of *ducks* and *waders* are always to be found. *Yellow wagtails* once nested here and it is a good area for *tree sparrows. Little terns*

WICKLOW

nest on this coast and in winter *snow buntings* are not uncommon on the shingle. From 'the breaches', where the water spills from the marsh into the sea, south to Newcastle railway station is usually a quiet area for birds but from Newcastle south to **Broad Lough** is much better. Watch for *reed warblers* in summer. *Marsh harriers* are more likely to be seen here than in most other parts of Ireland and *osprey* and *black kite* have been seen. Broad Lough holds *ducks*, some wild *swans* and a flock of *greylag geese*. *Geese* are seen in small numbers all along this coast and can include *white-fronted* and *pink-footed geese*.

Wicklow Head, to the south of Wicklow town, is a good migration watch-point. Seawatching has been carried out successfully from here: *shearwaters* and *skuas* can be seen in suitable weather conditions. But it is also a good place, one of the best on the east coast, for watching *passerine* migrants. *Partridges* still occur here and I know of birdwatchers who have travelled long distances to see the Wicklow Head *partridges*. Farther south, **Arklow Pond**, right in the town of Arklow, usually has *whooper swans* in winter. Offshore a large flock of *common scoters* spends the winter.

There are several wetlands worth visiting in inland Wicklow. Blessington reservoir is probably the best area, holding one of the largest flocks of *greylag geese* in the country. Up to 360 have been seen, but they move about the lake and into fields close to the shore. Very large numbers of *lesser black-backed gulls* roost on the lake in winter. The **Vartry reservoir** and the lakes at **Glendalough** occasionally have *whooper swans* but these lakes are deep and rather disappointing for birds. The woodlands of Wicklow, however, are usually very rewarding for the visiting birdwatcher, especially in summer. Go to the deciduous woods at the **Glen of the Downs**, and **Devil's Glen** near Ashford, **Glendalough**, **Powerscourt** or **Derrybawn Wood** near Laragh. These woods all hold nesting *blackcaps* and in most of them *wood warblers* sing annually in May. Whether they all breed or just sing briefly and move on is unknown. *Redstarts* also occur in some of these areas and other species which nest commonly just across the Irish Sea but have not been found breeding in Ireland could be found here in future. *Pied flycatchers* have been seen, though not proved to nest, and one might not be too surprised to find *firecrests* or *tree pipits* in summer in the area. As well as the old oakwoods, Wicklow has many plantations of conifers; the young plantations provide nesting sites for *hen harriers*. The mature plantations are difficult to birdwatch in, but *siskins* and *redpolls* can usually be found. Knowledge of the calls of these birds is helpful in tracing them.

On the open moorland *hen harriers* can frequently be seen hunting and *merlins*, which have decreased in recent years, can also be seen most days. *Red grouse* are still widespread though thinly spread. *Whinchats* nest among the younger plantations. On the scree slopes of rocky glens *ring ouzels* nest: the best place to see them is at the carpark at Baravore in **Glenmalure**. Again, sighting the bird is difficult unless you have a good ear for the bird's call. But the most spectacular bird of Wicklow is the *peregrine* which now nests widely in the mountains. Do not disturb them if you find a nest, for this is the centre of the Irish breeding population.

I cannot advise the birdwatcher on any particular part of Wicklow to visit in summer. The scarcer breeding birds are all sensitive to disturbance but the county is large and rewarding for the observer who is prepared to spend long hours in the field. There are undoubtedly discoveries to be made among the breeding birds, but hard work will be required to make them.

Peregrine falcon

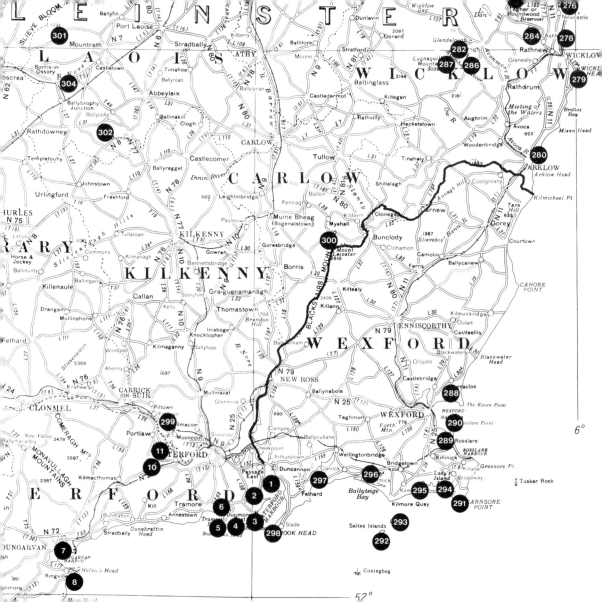

WEXFORD

Although it is a long way from Dublin, Wexford draws birdwatchers from the capital every weekend. Wexford's attractions are so great and so well known that it has been well watched for many years. A bird observatory was established on Great Saltee Island as long ago as 1950 and an annual report published with the *Irish Bird Report*. The Wexford Slobs were famous for many decades, especially among wildfowlers. More recently the establishment of a *wildfowl* reserve on the North Slob has attracted the general public in large numbers. *The Birds of Wexford* by Oscar J. Merne, a booklet published by Bord Fáilte in 1974, is the best guide to the county, though now out of print. More recently, an annual *Wexford Bird Report* has been published by the Irish Wildbird Conservancy. There are two books on the Saltees: *The Birds and Flowers of the Saltee Islands* by Ken Perry and Stephen Warburton, published in 1976, and *Saltees — Islands of Birds and Legends* by Richard Roche and Oscar Merne, published in 1977. There is an active branch of the IWC in Wexford town.

The **North Slob**, an area of land on the north side of Wexford Harbour reclaimed from the sea in the 1840s, contains the only wetland bird reserve with a full-time warden in the Republic. This reserve is owned jointly by the Forest and Wildlife Service and the IWC. Facilities are excellent for the visitor who wishes to watch the birds from the relative comfort of hides. Approach the reserve by turning right off the main Wexford–Gorey road about three kilometres north of Wexford town. The road is clearly signposted and leads to a hide overlooking a broad channel and, beyond this, a carpark, reception hall, warden's house and observation tower. Birdwatching is limited to the area around the observation tower and the hide overlooking the channel because the bulk of the 1000 hectares of the North Slob is private property. A leaflet is available at the reserve or from the IWC.

From the hide overlooking the channel good views can be had of *wigeon, teal, mallard, shoveler, coots* and, frequently, *spotted redshanks* and other *waders*. *White-fronted geese*, for which the Slob is famous, sometimes come down to the edge to wash. The North and South Slob together hold up to 7000 *Greenland white-fronted geese*, the highest wintering concentration in the world. From the top of the observation tower very good views can be had of flocks of several hundred of these birds. Usually a few *pink-footed*

WEXFORD

288. North Slob
289. South Slob
290. Rosslare
      back strand
291. Carnsore Point
292. Great Saltee
293. Little Saltee
294. Lady's Island Lake
295. Tacumshin Lake
296. The Cull
297. Bannow Bay
298. Hook Head

129

geese, Canada geese (including some very small birds), *barnacle geese* and in most winters a *snow goose* can be found among the *white-fronted geese,* and *brent geese* can be seen on the fields when high tide covers the sands of Wexford Harbour.

The Slobs hold many more birds than just the *geese* and *ducks*. Watch for *hen harriers, merlins* and *short-eared owls*. Look across Wexford Harbour from the observation tower. *Goldeneyes, red-breasted mergansers* and, sometimes, *slavonian* or *black-necked grebes* occur here.

Under no circumstances should visitors travel around the rest of the North Slob unless accompanied by the warden.

The **South Slob**, which was reclaimed shortly after the North Slob, is located on the south side of Wexford Harbour between Wexford town and Rosslare strand. It is a little smaller than the North Slob and, like it, has a wide, shallow channel running through it. The entire Slob is privately owned and permission to visit should be arranged through the warden of the North Slob in advance. To approach the South Slob, take the Rosslare road south from Wexford town and after three kilometres turn left where you see The Farmer's Kitchen public house. After a further kilometre turn left between two water-filled quarry holes. This road leads directly onto the South Slob.

The birds of the South Slob tend to be similar to those of the North Slob and at its north-east corner the South Slob adjoins portion of **Rosslare back strand** where *brent geese* and *waders* can be seen. However, the back strand can be approached much more conveniently by driving to Rosslare Strand village and taking the road to Rosslare Point. As well as providing a vantage point for viewing the birds of the strand, the point is also a convenient site for searching the harbour for *terns* in summer or *divers* and *grebes* in winter.

Carnsore Point, the south-east corner of Ireland, is rather too extensive to be a good migration watchpoint. *Passerine* birds disperse rapidly and there is very little of the funnelling effect which leads to concentrations of birds on narrow headlands.

This effect can be seen to its best advantage on offshore islands and nowhere in Ireland better than on **Great Saltee** island where the first Irish Bird Observatory was established in 1950. The two Saltees, Great and Little Saltee, lie a few kilometres south of Kilmore Quay and, while both have interesting *seabird* colonies, it is Great Saltee which is famous for migrants. Landing is usually from a fishing boat hired at Kilmore Quay and can only be attempted in relatively calm conditions as the landing place is on a boulder beach on the north shore. The beach runs the length of the north shore but there are steep cliffs on the other side. The island is about two kilometres long and one kilometre wide. A stone farmhouse stands near the landing and has a clump of trees and small garden beside it. To the east is situated a small bungalow. There is no regular ferry service to the island and a boat must be specially arranged in advance.

During the spring period of April to mid-May the island can hold hundreds, even thousands, of migrant *passerines*. During the autumn months of August to October numbers are smaller but the unexpected can always appear. A total of 209 species was recorded on the island by the bird observatory which operated from 1950 to 1962. Perhaps the most spectacular sight of all for a visitor is the huge concentration of breeding *seabirds* in summer. Many thousands of *guillemots*, *razorbills* and *kittiwakes* nest on the cliffs. Over 1000 pairs of *puffins* nest in burrows above the cliffs and the top of the island is covered with breeding *gulls*. A small colony of *gannets* occupies the southern tip of the island. An introductory leaflet on the Great Saltee is available from the IWC.

The **Little Saltee** is difficult to land on and has fewer nesting *seabirds*, though it does have a large colony of *cormorants*, a species which does not nest on the Great Saltee. The Great Saltee was acquired by Michael Neale in 1943 and, some years later, the Little Saltee passed into the same hands. Shortly after buying the larger island he adopted the title 'Prince of the Saltees' and erected a stone throne, an obelisk and a flagstaff. Permission should always be sought from Prince Michael Neale by anyone wishing to stay overnight.

Between Carnsore Point and Kilmore Quay lie two brackish lagoons, **Lady's Island Lake** and Tacumshin Lake. Lady's Island Lake is separated from the sea by a shingle bank which is cut open annually to permit water to flow out, but gales close it quickly. The north side of the lake has broad areas of sand and mud exposed after drainage where *waders* can be seen. At the south-east corner of the lake is a small lake and marsh known as Ring Marsh where many *ducks* and some *great crested grebes* nest. In winter the lake is an important place for wintering *wildfowl*. In summer *black-headed gulls, Sandwich terns* and *roseate terns* nest on the islands in the lake.

A couple of kilometres west of Lady's Island Lake and seven kilometres east of Kilmore Quay lies **Tacumshin Lake**. The lake has three islands, one at the eastern end and two in the west. When the water level is low, as it frequently is in summer and autumn, there are extensive areas of mud exposed around these islands known as 'The Patches'. In the late 1970s and early 1980s this area became one of the best in Europe for seeing vagrant *waders* from North America and, indeed, from Europe among the flocks which broke their migratory journeys here. At some weekends up to fifty birdwatchers could be seen, searching among the *waders* for rarities. But Tacumshin is more than just a place for rare birds: it holds all the common *ducks, waders, gulls* and *terns* at the right time of the year and is worth visiting at any time. In winter look out for *brent geese*, usually on the saltmarsh at The Patches.

Access is via Tomhaggard, a small village off the main road from Wexford to Kilmore Quay. Take the first turn left about a kilometre after passing through Tomhaggard and follow the narrow lane down to the marsh. This portion is known as The White Hole. Search the area carefully and then walk eastwards along the shore of Tacumshin Lake to look across to The Patches. Later, return to Tomhaggard and turn right instead of returning to Wexford. After a kilometre turn right down a narrow lane past a ruined castle to the shore. Here you can get good views across the mudflats.

West of Kilmore Quay is a long, narrow inlet known as **The Cull** which can be watched from The Cull Bank near Killag,

about three kilometres north of Kilmore Quay. Turn left at Killag for Duncormick and follow the road for two kilometres to Park where the road turns right. Take a left turn here down a narrow lane which leads to The Cull Bank. The estuary holds up to 5000 *waders* including *oystercatchers, black-tailed godwits, bar-tailed godwits, redshanks, knots* and *dunlin*. Some *white-fronted geese* occur. **Bannow Bay**, a large, open bay running for about seven kilometres from Wellingtonbridge to the open sea, is of interest during the winter for the large number of *wildfowl* and *waders* it holds. Because the mudflats are so extensive it is often difficult to get reasonable views of the birds. The best place to see large numbers of birds is from the road between Wellingtonbridge and Duncormick just south of Wellingtonbridge. At high tide, or for an hour either side of high tide, the majority of *waders* and *wigeon* in the bay can be seen at the Clonmines saltmarsh or on the surrounding mud.

Hook Head, a long, low promontory at the western side of Bannow Bay is a good site for watching *passerine* migrants or *seabirds*. Drive right to the tip where the ancient lighthouse is an obvious landmark. The best conditions for seawatching are in south-westerly gales. Land migrants occur in large numbers after spring or autumn 'falls' and can include rare species such as *firecrests, woodchat shrikes* and *icterine warblers*. The best places for migrants are south of a line from Churchtown to Slade and, in the right conditions, usually after south-easterly winds, hedges here can be full of *blackcaps, chiffchaffs, goldcrests* and other migrants. A booklet *Birds of Hook Head* by J.K. Lovatt was published by the IWC in 1985 and is an invaluable guide.

Brent goose

KILKENNY

The inland counties of south Leinster are very much understudied by birdwatchers. Not many important bird haunts are known but there are undoubtedly discoveries to be made. Kilkenny has a variety of habitats but very few places where many water birds occur. **Tibberoughney Marsh** in south Kilkenny on the edge of the River Suir is an exception. The area is best approached from the village of Tibberoughney about two kilometres south-east of Piltown. It consists of a large marsh with flooded areas of pasture. In winter the *greylag geese* which feed at Coolfin roost here. *Mallard, teal, tufted duck, wigeon* and *whooper* and *Bewick's swans* all occur.

The county has excellent woodland bird habitat in a variety of locations but especially in the river valleys. *Jays, barn owls, kestrels* and *sparrowhawks* are all resident and fairly widespread though the distribution of *barn owls* is not well known. In winter flocks of *lapwings, golden plover, redwings* and *fieldfares* are widespread.

CARLOW

In general the birds of Carlow are very similar to those of Kilkenny, but the county does have a branch of the IWC. The only medium-sized body of standing water is an artificial pond at **Oak Park**, owned by the Agricultural Institute, where *mallard, teal, tufted duck* and *pochard* can all be seen. An interesting bird habitat, well worth visiting, is the top of the Mount Leinster chain of mountains where *hen harriers* and *red grouse* breed.

KILKENNY

299. Tibberoughney Marsh

CARLOW

300. Oak Park

LAOIS

Laois has a wide range of habitats but few lakes. The **Slieve Bloom Mountains** hold a relatively rich breeding bird fauna. The best place to visit is The Cut where the road runs across the summit of the range. Look out for *hen harriers* in particular. Laois has one important wetland, the '**Curragh**' between Rathdowney and Durrow. This is a stretch of rough meadow along the River Erkina south of Ballacolla. It is important for the occurrence of a small wintering population of *Greenland white-fronted geese* which move about to nearby areas as well as feeding in the callows at this site. Other places where the *geese* may be seen include **Lough Annaghmore** and the flats beside the **River Nore near Borris-in-Ossory.**

KILDARE

Prosperous reservoir, the source of the Grand Canal, is an interesting lake for breeding birds. Large numbers of *black-headed gulls* breed here and smaller numbers of *mallard, little grebes, snipe* and *redshanks*. There are many good areas in the county for our scarcer breeding birds. *Jays, blackcaps* and *whinchats* may all be found. An IWC branch covers north Kildare and part of west Dublin.

LAOIS

301. Slieve Bloom
      Mountains
302. The 'Curragh'
303. Lough Annaghmon
304. River Nore near
      Borris-in-Ossory

KILDARE

305. Prosperous reservoir

137

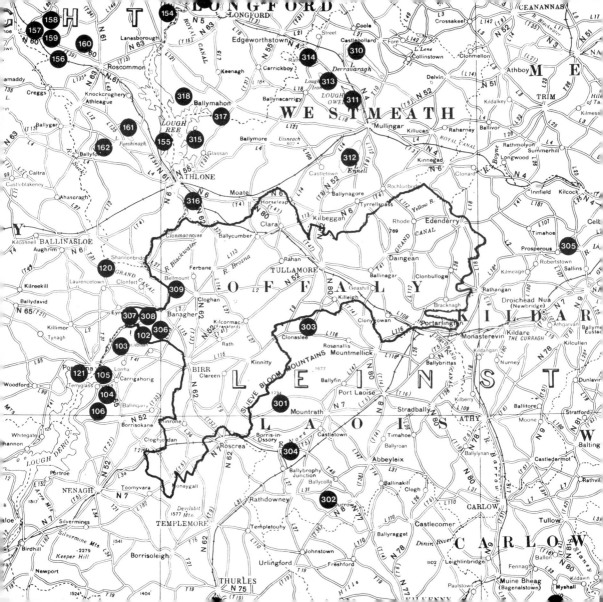

OFFALY

Offaly has one outstanding feature of significance for birds: it is bounded by the River Shannon. Several tributaries of the Shannon flow through the county and one of these, the **Little Brosna**, is an outstanding wetland by internationally accepted standards, though unfortunately not well known by Irish birdwatchers. The Little Brosna from New Bridge seven kilometres north-west of Birr to the junction with the Shannon at Meelick is a narrow river surrounded by low-lying pasture which floods in winter. The flooded callows provide safety and feeding for *wigeon, teal*, wild *swans* and *geese*. The edges of the floodwater and the surrounding farmland hold some of the largest flocks of *lapwing* and *golden plover* in the country. In among them are flocks of *curlews, black-tailed godwits* and *dunlins*.

The best way to approach the bird areas is to take the road from New Bridge along the north side of the Little Brosna and to walk down to the edge of the flooded callows. Walk the callows as far as **Cloghan Castle** for here the largest numbers of birds occur and they usually include several hundred *white-fronted geese*. The second largest flock in the country winters here: the largest is on the Wexford Slobs. Having worked the area thoroughly, and this will take much of the day, drive around to the Shannon at Lavagh and look across at **Big Island**

and **Friar's Island** where *ducks* and *geese* settle during days of intensive shooting.

At times the Little Brosna is extremely heavily shot, both from boats and the shore, but the area of floodwater is vast and the birds can settle out of range. Nevertheless, disturbance is substantial and, as a result, the birds are wary. But this is a magnificent place for watching *wildfowl* and *waders*, and for me is one of the most spectacularly wild places in the country.

The **River Shannon** from Clonmacnoise south to the junction with the Little Brosna holds several thousand *wigeon* and smaller numbers of *teal*, wild *swans* and a few *white-fronted geese* in winter. However, the roads do not run parallel to the Shannon so the area is difficult to watch. The best way to get near the birds is to approach at Clonmacnoise, Shannonbridge and occasional points further south where the road runs close to the river for a short spell. Efforts have been made to count the birds from the edge but without real success: the only way to assess the numbers is to take a light aircraft over the birds and count from the passenger's seat.

OFFALY

139

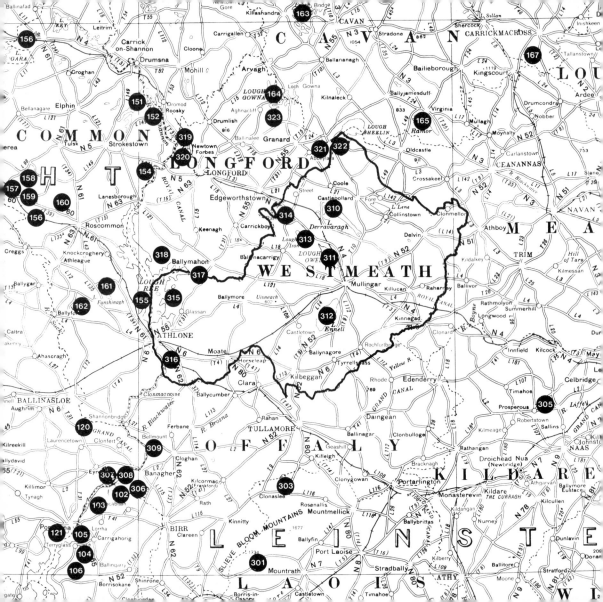

WESTMEATH

This is a county of scenic lakes, popular for shooting in summer and autumn, and packed with *duck* in winter. Many of the lakes are rarely watched, except by a handful of local ornithologists. Although the lakes appear superficially similar they hold quite different populations of birds.

Lough Derravaragh, north of Mullingar, is probably the best lake for birds: it is also the best known. Derravaragh is a rich, shallow, limestone lake on the River Inny system. Drainage of the River Inny some years ago lowered the water level exposing sandy and muddy banks at the north-west end and improving the feeding for *waders*. In early autumn a large post-breeding flock of *mallard* assembles to moult; from mid-August *pochards* arrive in large numbers, building up to a peak of 5000 – 6000 birds. Perhaps they moult here but nobody knows. A little later, in mid-October, *tufted ducks* arrive, building up to 2000 or so and a huge flock of *coots* peaks in November and December. The muddy edge of the lake is attractive fo passing *waders* like *wood sandpipers* and *ruffs* in autumn and rarities such as *pectoral sandpiper* have been seen.

Lough Owel and **Lough Ennel** are the two other large lakes in Westmeath. Lough Owel, which can be watched from the Dublin – Sligo road, has relatively larger numbers of *mallard, tufted ducks*

and *wigeon* than the other lakes and holds the largest flock of *shovelers* in Ireland. Lough Ennel is principally important for diving *ducks* and *coots*, but a flock of *white-fronted geese* uses fields at one corner. These *geese* also use **Lough Iron**, a smaller lake about two kilometres north-west of Lough Owel, which usually has a large wintering flock of *whooper swans* and good numbers of *ducks*. If you visit Lough Iron do not omit to visit **Glen Lough** as well. This lake, about five kilometres north-west of Lough Iron, holds few diving *ducks* but good numbers of surface feeders. It is perhaps the least known of these lakes.

Westmeath is bordered on its western edge by Lough Ree and the River Shannon. The shore of **Lough Ree** is not well known but good numbers of diving *duck* have been recorded. The **Shannon** just south of Athlone holds *wigeon* and wild *swans* but not in the same numbers as further south.

This is a particularly interesting county for the birdwatcher. For the resident of Dublin it is every bit as accessible as Dundalk Bay and much closer than the Wexford Slobs. The lakes in particular would probably repay much more watching.

WESTMEATH

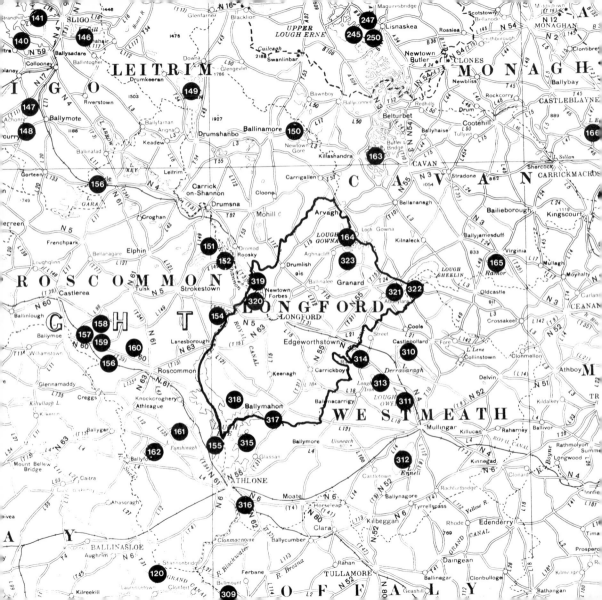

LONGFORD

Like Westmeath, Longford is a county of lakes and is bordered on its western edge by the River Shannon and Lough Ree. The mouth of the **River Inny** is good for both breeding and wintering birds. Look out for *black-tailed godwits* in autumn. The stretch at **Barley Harbour** also looks promising. **Lough Forbes** is a large Shannon lake north of Lough Ree edged with reeds and woodlands and of interest for woodland birds. **Castleforbes** demesne is a very important *white-fronted goose* wintering area. The river between Lough Forbes and Lough Ree appears to be less exciting for birds than much of the rest of the Shannon.

The best lake is **Lough Kinale** which at times has held large flocks of diving *ducks* and requires further study. Unfortunately, the adjoining **Lough Sheelin** is heavily polluted and holds few birds. **Lough Gowna** at the northern end of the county has an attractive woodland fringe and is probably a good *wildfowl* breeding area. Numbers in winter are not so high as at some of the other lakes.

LONGFORD

317. *River Inny*
318. *Barley Harbour*
319. *Lough Forbes*
320. *Caslteforbes demesne*
321. *Lough Kinale*
322. *Lough Sheelin*
323. *Lough Gowna*

About the Irish Wildbird Conservancy

The Irish Wildbird Conservancy is the largest voluntary organisation in Ireland concerned solely with wildlife conservation. One of its most important tasks is the management of reserves to protect wild birds and their habitats. Members may take part in national bird surveys to provide the facts on which conservation is based. The IWC is a recognised charity supported by over 4000 members.

There is a network of local IWC branches throughout Ireland. Each branch has frequent film shows, talks and outings in which members may participate. The annual journal *Irish Birds* (incorporating the Irish Bird Report) is published by the IWC. Members receive free a quarterly newsletter full of information and photographs. A special junior section, known as the Irish Young Ornithologists, runs activities for members under eighteen years.

On joining all new members receive a free badge or car sticker, an introductory booklet on *Beginning Birdwatching* and a twelve-page checklist of Irish birds. For further details of membership write to Department C, **Irish Wildbird Conservancy, Southview, Church Road, Greystones, Co. Wicklow. Telephone: (01) 875759.**